# THE COVENANT

Transforming The Heart of Your Marriage

VANCE K. JACKSON, JR.

The Covenant: Transforming The Heart of Your Marriage.
ISBN: 978-1-7369832-1-8
Published by 5th Gen Publishing, LLC.
© 2021 Vance K. Jackson, Jr.
www.VanceKJackson.com

Printed in the United States of America. All rights reserved. No portion of this book may be reproduced, stored in a retrieval system, or transmitted in any form or by any means—electronic, mechanical, photocopy, recording, scanning, or other—except for brief quotations in critical reviews or articles, without the prior written permission of the publisher.

Scripture quotations taken from the Amplified® Bible (AMPC), Copyright © 1954, 1958, 1962, 1964, 1965, 1987 by The Lockman Foundation Used by permission. www.lockman.org

Scripture quotations from The Authorized King James Version (KJV). Rights in the Authorized Version in the United Kingdom are vested in the Crown. Reproduced by permission of the Crown's patentee, Cambridge University Press.

Scripture quotations marked (MSG) are taken from THE MESSAGE, copyright © 1993, 2002, 2018 by Eugene H. Peterson. Used by permission of NavPress, represented by Tyndale House Publishers. All rights reserved.

Scripture quotations marked (NIV) are taken from the Holy Bible, New International Version®, NIV®. Copyright © 1973, 1978, 1984, 2011 by Biblica, Inc.™ Used by permission of Zondervan. All rights reserved worldwide. www.zondervan.com The "NIV" and "New International Version" are trademarks registered in the United States Patent and Trademark Office by Biblica, Inc.™

Scripture quotations marked (NLT) are taken from the Holy Bible, New Living Translation, copyright © 1996, 2004, 2015 by Tyndale House Foundation. Used by permission of Tyndale House Publishers, Inc., Carol Stream, Illinois 60188. All rights reserved.

Library of Congress Cataloging-in-Publication Data

Library of Congress Control Number: 2021912962

# LOVE NOTE

*To my Nina,*

*Mere words cannot express how much you mean to me. It would take me more than a lifetime to pen words that would capture the adequate expression of my love for you.*

*You are more than my "good thing". You are my crown and Heaven's gift. You were crafted by the Hand of God for me. I couldn't have dreamed of a greater gift.*

*You are favor personified. Your beauty is unmatched. Your intellect is like no other. Wisdom drips from your lips. Excellence and grace clothe you. You inspire me daily.*

*I love you. I love our journey. I love us. Thank you for saying yes. I honor you. I adore you.*

*Forever yours,*
*Vance K. Jackson Jr.*

# TABLE OF CONTENTS

My Prayer For Your Marriage . . . . . . . . . . . . . . . . . . . . . . . . . . 1

**DAY 1**
The Garden: Where It All Started. . . . . . . . . . . . . . . . . . . . . 5

**DAY 2**
Protect The Ground of Your Marriage . . . . . . . . . . . . . . . . 9

**DAY 3**
Death Is a Process . . . . . . . . . . . . . . . . . . . . . . . . . . . . . . . . 13

**DAY 4**
Withering Is a Choice . . . . . . . . . . . . . . . . . . . . . . . . . . . . . 17

**DAY 5**
Let the Dead Bury the Dead . . . . . . . . . . . . . . . . . . . . . . . 21

**DAY 6**
Be Not Conformed . . . . . . . . . . . . . . . . . . . . . . . . . . . . . . . 25

**DAY 7**
Draw Near to God . . . . . . . . . . . . . . . . . . . . . . . . . . . . . . . 29

**DAY 8**
The Marital Bed Undefiled. A Living Sacrifice . . . . . . . . . . 33

**DAY 9**
A New Creature . . . . . . . . . . . . . . . . . . . . . . . . . . . . . . . . . 37

**DAY 10**
Sin Corrupts Your Harvest . . . . . . . . . . . . . . . . . . . . . . . . . 41

**DAY 11**
Forgive Freely . . . . . . . . . . . . . . . . . . . . . . . . . . . . . . . . . . . 45

**DAY 12**
Corrupt Communication . . . . . . . . . . . . . . . . . . . . . . . . . . 49

**DAY 13**
Lead Her in Love . . . . . . . . . . . . . . . . . . . . . . . . . . . . . . . .57

**DAY 14**
The Deep Wells of Communication . . . . . . . . . . . . . . . . . . . .63

**DAY 15**
Submission Is Not Bondage . . . It's Power . . . . . . . . . . . . . .69

**DAY 16**
Submission Is a Choice . . . . . . . . . . . . . . . . . . . . . . . . . .77

**DAY 17**
War Together. . . . . . . . . . . . . . . . . . . . . . . . . . . . . . . . .83

**DAY 18**
Kill the Snake . . . . . . . . . . . . . . . . . . . . . . . . . . . . . . . .89

**DAY 19**
Build Together . . . . . . . . . . . . . . . . . . . . . . . . . . . . . . .99

**DAY 20**
Send the Word . . . . . . . . . . . . . . . . . . . . . . . . . . . . . . .109

**DAY 21**
As for Me and My House . . . We Will Serve the Lord . . .113

# MY PRAYER FOR YOUR MARRIAGE

It is my earnest prayer that as you're reading this book, God leads and ministers to your heart. It is my prayer that God speaks directly to your circumstance and transforms the heart of your marriage.

It is also my prayer that your marriage is strengthened as you're reading the words contained in these pages. I pray that these words come alive within the walls of your marriage. I pray that your marriage is sharpened as you turn each page. I pray that God shifts and transforms your marriage and elevates your house to unprecedented levels.

It is my prayer that as you're reading this devotional, the infrastructure and foundation of your marriage are strengthened. I pray that God heals parts of your marriage that you didn't know needed to be healed.

This book was designed to strengthen, heal, and transform your marriage—it is also my deepest desire that God strengthens, heals, and transforms your heart. I pray that God leads and softens the ground of your heart. I pray that the ground of your heart becomes ripe and ready to receive God's Word.

It is my prayer that as you're reading this book with your spouse, God heals old wounds of the past. I pray that God restores families through the content enclosed in these pages. May God ignite your marriage for His Glory.

I'm praying for your marriage. I'm praying for your family. I'm praying for you. As you read this book, I pray that you discover new things about yourself, about your spouse, and about God. I pray that God reveals Himself to you in a fresh, new, and relevant way.

I pray that God reveals Himself to you and that your life is transformed from the inside out. I pray that your marital covenant is strengthened. More importantly, I pray that you draw closer to God and that you hunger and thirst after Him and His never-changing Word. Let God lead your heart as you read the words enclosed in these pages.

Be Blessed,
*Vance K. Jackson*

## Day 1

# THE GARDEN: WHERE IT ALL STARTED

*And the Lord God formed man of the dust of the ground, and breathed into his nostrils the breath of life; and man became a living soul.*

GENESIS 2:7 KJV

Let's go back to the beginning, where it all started, in Genesis and the Garden of Eden. Genesis 2:8 KJV declares, "And the Lord God planted a garden eastward in Eden; and there he put the man whom he had formed." Notice, in this verse, that God created the Garden of Eden first, and then He placed man to steward over everything in it. Man did not create the Garden—God created the Garden. Man did not plant the Garden—God planted the Garden. God created the Garden and everything that was in it.

The Garden of Eden was perfect. The Garden was planted by God and was given to man, by God, to steward, cover, and protect every aspect of it. The Garden of Eden was man's God-given assignment. The Garden was man's platform. God prepared the platform. God prepares platforms and assigns people where it pleases Him.

God plants and prepares gardens. Your marital covenant is a God-prepared Garden. The borders of your Garden belong to God and He assigned you to steward it well. Your marriage was created by God. Marriage is more than a carnal platform. Marriage is more than a man-made contract or institution. Marriage is a God-ordained Covenant between God, man, and woman.

The institution of marriage was created by God Himself. Genesis 2:18 KJV declares, "And the Lord God said, It is not good that the man should be alone; I will make him an help meet for him." God created your spouse, and through the covenant of marriage, it is your responsibility to love your spouse as God leads your heart. Choose to love your spouse. Choose to reflect the Heart and Character of God in the confines of your marriage.

Genesis 2:8 AMPC declares, "And the Lord God planted a garden toward the east, in Eden [delight]; and there He put the man whom He had formed (framed, constituted)." Notice that the Amplified Version declares that Eden was a "Delight." According to Strong's Concordance, the definition of Eden (H5731) means "Pleasure." God created the Garden of Eden as a place of peace, pleasure, and delight. Marriage was created by God to be a place of peace, pleasure, and delight.

God wants your marriage to be whole. God wants your marriage to be healed. God wants your marriage to be sound. God wants your marriage to be fruitful. The Garden of Eden was full—nothing was lacking. The Garden of Eden was full of peace. The Garden of Eden was full of riches. God designed every aspect of the Garden of Eden to reflect His Peace and Wholeness. God wants your marriage to reflect His complete Peace and Wholeness. The Garden of Eden was whole and perfect until sin entered. Where did sin enter your garden?

## COUPLES' PRAYER

Father God, in the Name of Jesus, we thank You for our marriage. Father, we thank You for each other. Father, we thank You for sending Your Son, Jesus Christ, to die for our sin. His Blood washes us. His Blood renews us. His Blood restores us.

Father, through Your Son, Jesus Christ, every generational cycle is broken. It is through Jesus Christ that our sins are washed away and every entanglement of sin is broken. Father, it is through Your Son, Jesus Christ, that our family is restored, healed, and made whole.

Father, we thank You for covering our marriage. We thank You for keeping Your Covenant with us. We surrender our marriage to You. We surrender our hearts to You. We submit our lives to You. We accept Jesus Christ as our Lord and Savior and we invite You into our home. Lead and direct our thoughts. Guide our path. Father, lead our ways and guide our actions. Lord, lead our marriage. Father, we surrender our family to You.

In Jesus' Name. Amen.

## ACTION

- Ask God to lead your marriage and to soften your heart as you read this devotional.
- Choose to develop a prayer life together. Strengthen your marriage through prayer. Pray together.
- Take some time today to outline and identify some areas of your marriage that need to be strengthened.

---------- Day 2 ----------

## PROTECT THE GROUND OF YOUR MARRIAGE

*And the Lord God took the man, and put him into the garden of Eden to dress it and to keep it. And the Lord God commanded the man, saying, Of every tree of the garden thou mayest freely eat: But of the tree of the knowledge of good and evil, thou shalt not eat of it: for in the day that thou eatest thereof thou shalt surely die.*

GENESIS 2:15-17 KJV

Where did sin enter the borders of your marriage? What did God tell you not to touch? In Genesis 2:17 KJV, God told Adam not to eat from a specific tree, "But of the tree of the knowledge of good and evil, thou shalt not eat of it: for in the day that thou eatest thereof thou shalt surely die." When God commands you not to touch something — do not touch it. Choose to obey God.

When God commands you not to touch, watch, or connect with something or someone that's not like Him — do not give in to the lust of the flesh. Choose to follow God's Word. Choose to obey God's Voice. Obey His Instruction. Submit to His Command and let your home and marriage flourish. What have you touched that God has told you not to touch? What have you entertained that God has told you not to entertain?

What's done in secret, God will bring it to light. Let God's Word shine on every area of your life. Let God's Word shine in every area of your marriage. Let His Word expose every hidden trap. Let His Power deliver you from every hidden secret. Let His Word deliver you from every addiction and bondage. Let His Word transform you. Let His Word make you whole.

When you surrender your life to Christ, He will remove the taste of lust, deception, deceit, perversion, and manipulation from your life. Let Christ till your heart's soil and cultivate the ground of your marriage. Let God remove what's not like Him. What's tainting the ground of your heart?

Jeremiah 4:3 KJV declares, "For thus saith the Lord to the men of Judah and Jerusalem, Break up your fallow ground, and sow not among thorns." Break up your own fallow ground. According to Strong's Concordance, the Hebrew word for Fallow is *niyr* (H5215), which means "Untilled." Let His Word till the ground of your heart. Let His Word cultivate the ground of your marriage. Let His Word break up the untilled, unfruitful, and unproductive parts of your life. Let His Word cultivate and nourish every aspect of your family, life, and marriage.

Hebrews 4:12 AMPC declares, "For the Word that God speaks is alive and full of power [making it active, operative, energizing, and effective]; it is sharper than any two-edged sword, penetrating to the dividing line of the breath of life (soul) and [the immortal] spirit, and of joints and marrow [of the deepest parts of our nature], exposing and sifting and analyzing and judging the very thoughts and purposes of the heart." Let God's Word sift and search every part of your heart. Let His Word sink deep into the very fabric and foundation of your marriage. His Word is alive, and is active, and will energize and strengthen the infrastructure of your home and marriage. Surrender to God. Choose to surrender to His Word.

## COUPLES' PRAYER

Father God, in the Name of Jesus, we thank You for our marriage. We thank You for resting in our home. Father, we declare that Your Peace rests here. Father, we declare that Your Security rests here.

Financial stability rests in our home. Father, we thank You for leading and guiding every aspect of our marriage. Father, we ask that You guide our thoughts and actions. We declare that You are the Lord over our hearts. Lord, let our marriage reflect You in private and in public.

Father, in the Name of Jesus, we crush anything that's not like You. Father, we renounce any activity and conduct that's not like You. Father, in the Name of Jesus, we surrender every aspect of our marriage over to You.

In Jesus' Name. Amen.

## ACTION

- Take some time today to read His Word together. (Suggested Reading: Ephesians 5)
- Remember the list that you made on Day 1? (The areas that need strengthening within your marriage.) Find some Scriptures that align with the items on your list.

- Meditate and focus on a few of these Scriptures throughout the day together.
- Call your spouse throughout the day and pray together. If you're unable to talk to your spouse on the phone, choose to pray for one another during your lunch break, or on your way to work, or before a meeting.
- Keep your spouse at the forefront of your mind. Be intentional and pray for your spouse.

# Day 3

# DEATH IS A PROCESS

*But of the tree of the knowledge of good and evil, thou shalt not eat of it: for in the day that thou eatest thereof thou shalt surely die.*

GENESIS 2:17 KJV

In Genesis 2:17, God outlines the reward or the consequence of sin. God tells Adam, "Thou shalt surely die." Death is a process. Adam did not die instantly, once he disobeyed God, he began to wither. After sin was introduced, Adam began to wither spiritually, physically, mentally, emotionally, and financially. Disobedience introduces decay.

Don't let your destiny decay. Don't forfeit your God-given Promise through disobedience or neglect. Don't forfeit your promotion by disobeying God's Voice. Don't forfeit your enlargement and expansion due to your disobedience or slothful obedience.

Disobedience delays destiny. Disobedience corrupts the soil of your heart and character. Disobedience disrupts peace. Disobedience breeds and cultivates an environment of rebellion and frustration.

If you've disobeyed God, if you've walked away from His Commands, choose to repent and turn back to God. Repentance reverses curses and breaks generational cycles. Proverbs 1:23 AMPC declares, "If you will turn (repent) and give heed to my reproof, behold, I [Wisdom] will pour out my spirit upon you, I will make my words known to you." Choose to repent and turn to God.

According to Strong's Concordance, the Hebrew word for Repent is *shuwb* (H7725), which means "To return or to turn back." Turn back to God. When you repent, you are turning away from the old way of doing things and embracing God's Way of doing things. When you repent, you are turning away from the old and surrendering to the new. Crucify your flesh and surrender to Christ.

Romans 6:6 KJV declares, "Knowing this, that our old man is crucified with him, that the body of sin might be destroyed, that henceforth we should not serve sin." When you are in Christ, you do not have to serve sin. When you serve Christ, you do not have to be a slave to sin. Crucify the old man and let Christ come alive in you.

According to Strong's Concordance, the Greek word for Crucify is *stauroō* (G4717), which means "To stake or to drive down stakes." Choose to crucify your flesh with the Word of God. Stake down sin with His Word. Let His Word crucify sin in every area of your life. Let His Word crush sin in every area of your marriage. Surrender to God.

Surrender to His Way of doing things. Surrender your marriage to God and let the old things go. Let the old ways die. Crush sin by surrendering to God. "Submit yourselves therefore to God. Resist the devil, and he will flee from you." James 4:7 KJV

## COUPLES' PRAYER

Father God, in the Name of Jesus, we thank You for our marriage. We thank You for Your Son, Jesus Christ. We thank You, that through His shed Blood, we have access to freedom.

Through the shed Blood of Jesus Christ, we have access to Your forgiveness. Through Christ, we are set free from the bondage of the past and the entanglement of sin. Through the shed Blood of Jesus Christ, we are set free.

Through the shed Blood of Jesus Christ, addiction has no power, pride has no place, and stubbornness has no authority — in Christ we are set free. Father, in the Name of Jesus Christ, we repent of any sin that we've committed against You. We turn from our ways and turn to You.

Father, in You, there is victory. Father, through Your Son, Jesus Christ, we are made new and every generational cycle is broken. Through the shed Blood of Jesus Christ, every generational curse is destroyed. Through the shed Blood of Jesus Christ, every generational pattern is dismantled. Lord, we are free in You.

Our marriage is strengthened in You. Our marriage is set free in You. Father, You are our True and Living God and we will serve no other. You are Lord over our house. Father, You are Lord over our marriage, and we surrender to You — forever.

In Jesus' Name. Amen.

## ACTION

▸ As a couple, make a conscious effort to take time today to read His Word together. Unity brings peace.

- Decide not to blame each other for past mistakes, sins, failures, and shortcomings. Let the past go and surrender completely to Christ.
- Be intentional and pray for your spouse throughout the day. Build up your prayer life together.

## Day 4

# WITHERING IS A CHOICE

*Abide in me, and I in you. As the branch cannot bear fruit of itself, except it abide in the vine; no more can ye, except ye abide in me. I am the vine, ye are the branches: He that abideth in me, and I in him, the same bringeth forth much fruit: for without me ye can do nothing. If a man abide not in me, he is cast forth as a branch, and is withered; and men gather them, and cast them into the fire, and they are burned.*

JOHN 15:4–6 KJV

Abide in Christ. Let God's Word burn away everything that's not like Him within the walls of your marriage. According to Strong's Concordance, the Greek word for Abide is *menō* (G3306), which means "To remain." Choose to remain in Christ. Allow every aspect of your marriage to abide in Him. Let your heart dwell in His Word. Choose to obey His Voice and follow His Instruction. Let your marriage abide in Him.

Deuteronomy 28:1–2 KJV declares, "And it shall come to pass, if thou shalt hearken diligently unto the voice of the Lord thy God, to observe and to do all his commandments which I command thee this day, that the Lord thy God will set thee on high above all nations of the earth: And all these blessings shall come on thee, and overtake thee, if thou shalt hearken unto the voice of the Lord thy God." When you diligently follow Christ and heed to His Instruction, Deuteronomy 28 declares that God will set you high above all the nations of the Earth.

Promotion comes as a result of your submission. Enlargement comes as a result of your surrendering. Expansion is a fruit of submission. As a couple, choose to break the yoke of generational bondage, cycles, and barriers by surrendering to His Word.

His Word has power. His Word is Power and can break through anything that opposes or hinders your marriage from being fruitful and successful. 1 Peter 5:7 KJV declares, "Casting all your care upon him; for he careth for you." The Amplified Version expounds upon 1 Peter 5:7 AMPC in the following manner, "Casting the whole of your care [all your anxieties, all your worries, all your concerns, once and for all] on Him, for He cares for you affectionately and cares about you watchfully. [Ps. 55:22.]"

God cares for you. God wants you to succeed. God wants your marriage to succeed. He wants you to thrive and not wither. God does not want your marriage to wither. God doesn't want you to wither. Withering is a choice.

Deuteronomy 30:19 KJV declares, "I call heaven and earth to record this day against you, that I have set before you life and death, blessing and cursing: therefore choose life, that both thou and thy seed may live:" God has set before you a choice — you have the choice to surrender to God and follow His Word, or you can surrender to the entanglements of the world and wither in the wilderness.

It's your choice. You can choose to wither or you can choose to let His Word come alive in the heart of your marriage. "Stand fast therefore in the liberty wherewith Christ hath made us free, and be not entangled again with the yoke of bondage." Galatians 5:1 KJV. Choose to be set free. Be not entangled in the yoke and bondage of the past.

## A HUSBAND'S PRAYER

Father God, in the Name of Jesus, I thank You for my wife. Father, I thank You that You have made her in Your image. Father, I thank You that she is a woman after Your Heart.

Father, I thank You for her wisdom, I thank You for her insight. Father, I thank You that she is a daughter after Your Own Heart. Father, there is no one like her.

Father, I thank You that my house is a place of peace. Father, I thank You that she is a reflection of Your Love and Character. My heart safely trusts in her. Lord, we submit to You. Father, our house trusts in You. Father, we choose to obey You. Lord, lead the heart of our house in every season of our lives.

In Jesus' Name. Amen.

## A WIFE'S PRAYER

Father God, in the Name of Jesus, I thank You for my husband. Father, I thank You that You have made him in Your image. Father, I thank You that he is a son after Your Heart.

Father, I thank You for his wisdom, I thank You for his leadership. Father, I thank You for his understanding. Father, I thank

You that he is a husband after Your Own Heart. Father, there is no one like him.

Father, I thank You that our house is a place of peace. Father, I thank You that he is a reflection of Your Character and my heart safely trusts in him. Father, we choose to submit to You. Lord, our house trusts You.

Father, continue to lead the heart of our house in every season of our lives. Lord, we surrender to You.

In Jesus' Name. Amen.

## ACTION

- 1 Peter 5:7 KJV declares, "Casting all your care upon him; for he careth for you." Choose to cast your cares, worries, desires, and anxiety over to God. Give it over to God. Whatever that "it" may be — choose to deliberately give "it" over to Him.
- Make a list of your cares, worries, desires, and anxieties and deliberately cast them over to God.
- Decide not to blame each other for the past. Choose to surrender your thoughts, cares, and desires over to Christ daily.
- Your spouse is not your enemy. Redirect your frustrations and pray for one another. Choose not to war against each other. Redirect your focus and war together.

# Day 5

## LET THE DEAD BURY THE DEAD

*Jesus said unto him, Let the dead bury their dead: but go thou and preach the kingdom of God.*

LUKE 9:60 KJV

It's time to bury the past. Let the past go and move forward in Christ. Choose to follow Christ. Let Christ lead your heart. Let His Word lead your home. Let His Power pierce and penetrate every area of your heart and home. When you are in Christ, your life becomes brand new. The past is history and the future is bright in Him.

Surrender to God and let the heart of your marriage follow His Heartbeat. Let His Word become the rhythm and flow of your home. Choose to surrender every aspect of your life, family, and marriage over to Christ. There is no one like Him. Choose to put the past and the old patterns away and let Christ establish a new pattern through your marriage. Choose to be the example for generations to follow.

Luke 9:59–60 AMPC declares, "And He said to another, Become My disciple, side with My party, and accompany Me! But he replied, Lord, permit me first to go and bury (await the death of) my father. But Jesus said to him, Allow the dead to bury their own dead; but as for you, go and publish abroad throughout all regions the kingdom of God." Jesus presented this man with a choice. Jesus declared, to this man, "Become My disciple, side with My party, and accompany Me!"

Whose side are you on? When you choose to side with Christ, the old way of doing things die off. As you surrender to Christ, your heart changes, your taste changes — you change. When you are in Christ, He begins to mature you and develop you. When you choose to follow Christ, and become His Disciple, your desires change and you don't want to cling to the lusts of the world. When you accept Jesus Christ, as your Lord and Savior, your life begins to transform from the inside out. Before God transforms your marriage, He transforms your heart. Let God transform your heart.

Let God heal your heart. Let the fruit of His Word radiate into the walls of your marriage. Let His Word be revealed in every aspect of your character and marriage. Let His Heart be revealed through you. Let His Love lead you and guide you. You cannot treasure what the world treasures.

Let His Word penetrate through every interaction that you have with others — including how you handle your family, friends, co-workers, and your spouse. Handle your spouse with grace. Handle the heart of your spouse with love. Your spouse is not the enemy.

As you submit to Christ, let His Power bind you and your spouse together as one. Submit your heart to Christ and you will not fail. Let Christ handle the heart of your marriage and you'll find good success. Choose the path of life. Choose His Path. His Word is life. "Jesus saith unto him, I am the way, the truth, and the life: no man cometh unto the Father, but by me." John 14:6 KJV. "It is the spirit that quickeneth; the flesh profiteth nothing:

the words that I speak unto you, they are spirit, and they are life." John 6:63 KJV.

According to Strong's Concordance, the Greek word for Dead is *nekros* (G3498), which means "One that has breathed his last, lifeless, deceased, departed, one whose soul is in heaven or in hell, destitute of life, or without life." As we unpack what Jesus declared in Luke 9:59–60 KJV to this man, we notice that Jesus was not being harsh to this man's desire to bury his father, but rather, Jesus declares in this passage, "Let the dead bury their dead: but go thou and preach the kingdom of God." Luke 9:60 KJV. When you dig deeper into this passage, Jesus declares something deeper than physically burying the dead.

According to Strong's Concordance, the Greek word *nekros* (G3498) also means "Spiritually dead, destitute of a life that recognizes and is devoted to God, inactive as respects doing right, destitute of force or power, inactive, and inoperative." Let the dead bury the dead. Let the inoperative bury the inoperative. Let the inactive bury the inactive. Let the destitute of power bury the powerless. Let the spiritually dead bury the spiritually dead. As for you and your house — choose to follow Christ.

Sometimes, you have to let the dead bury the dead. Let Christ lead your heart. Become His Disciple and let His Power lead your pathway. Surrender your heart to Christ and let Christ lead your marriage. Follow His Way. Follow His Lively Pattern and get His Results.

Maybe you're trying to fix your marriage with dead things, old ideas, and old frameworks. God is the Architect of marriage. He is the Architect of Love. God is Love. Let God do a new thing. Surrender to Him. Follow His Way. Become His Disciple. Become a disciplined one — a submitted one. Submit your heart to God and let Christ lead your path.

"Behold, I will do a new thing; now it shall spring forth; shall ye not know it? I will even make a way in the wilderness, and rivers in the desert." Isaiah 43:19 KJV. Let God do a new thing within the walls of your marriage.

## Day 6

# BE NOT CONFORMED

*And be not conformed to this world: but be ye transformed by the renewing of your mind, that ye may prove what is that good, and acceptable, and perfect, will of God.*

ROMANS 12:2 KJV

Submit your heart and your marriage to God. Leave the past behind you. Leave the ways of the world behind you. It's time to move forward in everything that Christ has for you. God wants you to conquer new territories for Him. God wants to transform you. He wants to transform your family. God wants to transform a generation — through you.

Your marriage is an example of God's Love on Earth. Your marriage sets the pattern. Your marriage sets the tone of your family. You have the choice. Your marriage can either become a Godly example and pattern of success or it can wither in the wilderness by surrendering to the things and ways of this world. Choose to surrender to Christ. Choose life. Choose His Way.

According to Strong's Concordance, the Greek word for Conform is *syschēmatizō* (G4964), which means "To conform one's self (i.e., one's mind and character) to another's pattern, (fashion one's self according to)." You can choose to pattern your mind after the world's way of doing things or you can choose to follow Christ and let His Power transform you — forever.

According to Strong's Concordance, the Greek word for Transform is *metamorphoō* (G3339), which means "To change into another form, to transform, or to transfigure." When you choose to submit to Christ, you'll change into another form. When you pattern yourself after His Word, you'll begin to transform from the inside out. Transformation happens from the inside out. Manipulation happens from the outside in.

When you try to change or transform by your own power or in your own strength, you're manipulating others into thinking that a change has taken place on the inside, when really, it's just a facade. Facades fade away. True heart transformation comes from God.

When God transforms you, you'll change into another man — a man after His Heart. When Christ leads and orders your steps, the things that you used to do — you will not have a desire to do them anymore. The desires, cravings, and appetite that you used to have, will fade away. "When I was a child, I spake as a child, I understood as a child, I thought as a child: but when I became a man, I put away childish things." 1 Corinthians 13:11 KJV.

Transformation is a process. When you accept Jesus Christ as your Lord and Savior, you are changed instantly. When you accept Christ, your spiritual DNA instantly changes. Now, your flesh has to catch up with Whom your heart just accepted.

God transforms you, but you must choose to obey. God accepts you, but your body must submit and surrender. God embraces you and sees you through the Blood of His Son, Jesus Christ, but you must choose to put off the old man. The Good News is that you do not have to put away the former things on your own or in your own strength — that's why we have a Savior.

Jesus Christ did not only die for your sins but according to Matthew 1:23 KJV, Jesus Christ is also called Emmanuel, being interpreted, "God with us". God is with you. God is with your family. God is with your marriage. Jesus Christ wants you to be healed, whole, and restored.

Like Paul, who was formerly Saul, your transformation can be instantaneous. And then, sometimes, transformations can take a little longer. Paul puts it this way in Romans 6:1–2 KJV, "What shall we say then? Shall we continue in sin, that grace may abound? God forbid. How shall we, that are dead to sin, live any longer therein?" When you are in Christ, you are dead to sin. You have the choice to not live in sin. When you are in Christ, you have the choice to not live in the bondage of the past. Be not entangled by the lusts of the past. Choose Christ. You have the choice.

## COUPLES' PRAYER

Father God, in the Name of Jesus, we surrender to You. We accept Your Son, Jesus Christ as our Lord and Savior. We submit to Your Way of doing things. Father, we surrender our hearts to You. Father, we surrender our lives to You. Father, there is no one like You in all the Earth.

Father, our family surrenders to You. You are the Lord over our hearts, our lives, our minds, our thoughts, actions, and decisions. Father, we submit and surrender to You — forever.

In Jesus' Name. Amen.

## Day 7

# DRAW NEAR TO GOD

*Draw nigh to God, and he will draw nigh to you. Cleanse your hands, ye sinners; and purify your hearts, ye double minded.*

JAMES 4:8 KJV

Surrendering is a choice. Surrendering is a daily decision. When you submit your heart and life to God, it's a daily choice and a lifestyle. Surrendering is a daily act. Choose to surrender to God in every aspect of your life. 1 Peter 5:7 KJV declares, "Casting all your care upon him; for he careth for you." Choose to cast everything over to God. Don't let the cares of the world weigh you down. Don't let the things of this world stress you out. Decide to surrender to God.

Choose not to argue about the cares and worries of this world, ask God for wisdom, and surround yourself with wise counselors and advisors. Surrender your desires over to God and don't let anxiety rule over your heart. Practice living out 1 Peter 5:7 together. Cast your cares together.

Draw nigh to God and He will draw nigh to you. Draw close to God in every area of your heart. Ask God to give you wisdom when you don't have understanding. When you don't have the answers, choose to surrender to God. Choose to surrender to God — even when you think that you have the answers.

Proverbs 3:5–6 KJV commands us to, "Trust in the Lord with all thine heart; and lean not unto thine own understanding. In all thy ways acknowledge him, and he shall direct thy paths." The Amplified Version puts it this way, "Lean on, trust in, and be confident in the Lord with all your heart and mind and do not rely on your own insight or understanding. In all your ways know, recognize, and acknowledge Him, and He will direct and make straight and plain your paths." Proverbs 3:5–6 AMPC.

Choose to trust in the Lord. Choose to lean upon the Lord with all of your heart. Let your heart lean upon Him. Let His Word become the foundation and the bedrock of your life and your marriage. Draw near to Him. Draw close to Him together. If you don't have the answers, simply pray and ask God. James 1:5 KJV declares, "If any of you lack wisdom, let him ask of God, that giveth to all men liberally, and upbraideth not; and it shall be given him." God gives wisdom liberally. But you have to ask. Submit your heart to Him and allow God to soften every hardened area. You don't have all the answers. Ask God. Ask Him how to have a fruitful, full, and satisfying marriage.

Yes, Christ wants you to have a full, satisfying, and successful marriage. He wants your marriage to be a clean, romantic, happy, and exciting one. God wants you to be satisfied in every area of your life and marriage. 3 John 1:2 KJV declares, "Beloved, I wish above all things that thou mayest prosper and be in health, even as thy soul prospereth." God desires that your spiritual and natural life prospers — including your marriage.

Your marriage belongs to God. What you choose to do in private and in public — every aspect belongs to God. 3 John 1:2 AMPC declares, "Beloved, I pray that you may prosper in every way and [that your body] may keep well, even as [I know] your soul keeps well and prospers." Your body belongs to God. When you're married, your body is in covenant with your spouse. You both are one flesh. You both are submitted to each other and to Christ. You both belong to Christ.

Christ is Lord — and your spouse is not God. Your marriage, your covenant before God, is a reflection of God's Love in the Earth. We are to worship God and not our marriage. We are to worship God and not our spouse. We are to worship Christ and not our family. We are to worship God and surrender to His Way of doing things. Surrender your marriage over to Christ and watch God do miraculous things through you.

Let God's Way of doing things satisfy you. Let His Love be embedded throughout your marriage. Let His Love lead your marriage. Let His Love be reflected through you and your spouse. James 4:8 KJV declares, "Draw nigh to God, and he will draw nigh to you. Cleanse your hands, ye sinners; and purify your hearts, ye double minded." God will draw close to you as you draw close to Him. Choose to crave His Word. Choose to digest His Word daily.

The second part of James 4:8 KJV declares, "Draw nigh to God, and he will draw nigh to you. Cleanse your hands." According to Strong's Concordance, the Greek word for Cleanse is *katharizō* (G2511), which means "To make clean, cleanse from physical stains and dirt, to remove by cleansing; in a moral sense, to free from the defilement of sin and faults, to purify from wickedness, to free from the guilt of sin, to purify, to consecrate by cleansing or purifying, to consecrate, dedicate, or to pronounce clean in a Levitical sense."

When you surrender your marriage to God, He pronounces your marriage as clean. God cleanses your covenant when you surrender to Him. When you are in Christ, your marriage belongs to Him. You have the choice to either cleanse or defile your marriage. When you wash your marriage with the Word of God, you're choosing to cleanse it. When you choose to entangle in the lusts of the world and flesh, you defile it.

It's simple, the choice is up to you. Broken covenants defile the institution of marriage. Kept covenants keep marriages clean. You choose. Draw near to God and let Christ lead your marriage.

## Day 8

# THE MARITAL BED UNDEFILED. A LIVING SACRIFICE

*Marriage is honourable in all, and the bed undefiled: but whoremongers and adulterers God will judge.*

HEBREWS 13:4 KJV

When you surrender to Christ, you are declaring that every area of your life belongs to Him, including your members. Romans 12:1 KJV declares, "I beseech you therefore, brethren, by the mercies of God, that ye present your bodies a living sacrifice, holy, acceptable unto God, which is your reasonable service." Your body belongs to Him.

As a Christian, God declares, through Paul, in Romans 12:1 KJV, that we are to present our bodies as a living sacrifice, Holy, and acceptable unto God. If we are to present our bodies as a living sacrifice unto God, married or single, then how much more are we to present our marriages to God as a living, or continual sacrifice.

A living sacrifice is a daily decision. To present your body to God as a living or lively sacrifice is your reasonable service.

In other words, your life and lifestyle should reflect Christ continually. A living sacrifice is a continual presentation to God. Continually present your marriage as a present to God. Present your life as a present to God. Choose to present your private life and your public life as a present to God. What you choose to do in private and public should reflect the Heart and Character of God continually.

2 Timothy 3:16 KJV declares, "All scripture is given by inspiration of God, and is profitable for doctrine, for reproof, for correction, for instruction in righteousness:" Every scripture in the Bible was inspired by God and is profitable for doctrine or instruction. In other words, God's Word is profitable and is beneficial for those who want to live a life that is pleasing to Him and reflects His Word. His Word also corrects. Let God correct you. Let God prune your heart. Let God reprove and redirect you. If God's Word is beneficial for every aspect of our lives then His Word is also beneficial for our marriages.

The entire Song of Solomon is a reflection of God's Heart and Love for marriage. Through man, God wrote this book to show His Love in a Holy Union. Marriage is not boring. Marriage is a journey. The Song of Solomon is an expression of God's Love. In fact, all Scripture is a reflection of God's Love. And through marriage, we have the opportunity to express God's Love towards our spouse. We are reflectors of His Love.

So, if we are to reflect the Love of Christ within the borders of our marriage, then sexual acts expressed outside the borders of marriage are considered a trespass and violation against God. 1 Corinthians 6:18 KJV declares, "Flee fornication. Every sin that a man doeth is without the body; but he that committeth fornication sinneth against his own body." 1 Corinthians 6:18 AMPC expands upon this principle and states, "Shun immorality and all sexual looseness [flee from impurity in thought, word, or deed]. Any other sin which a man commits is one outside the body, but he who commits sexual immorality sins against his own body."

Choose to present your body and your sexual conduct as a living sacrifice, Holy, and acceptable unto God. Sex outside of marriage is a sin.

Additionally, 1 Corinthians 6:18 AMPC declares to, "Shun immorality and all sexual looseness [flee from impurity in thought, word, or deed]." The Bible declares for us to flee from impurity in thought, word, and deed. Present your thought-life as a living sacrifice, Holy, and acceptable unto God which is your reasonable service.

Christ, the Living Word — God in the flesh — declares in Matthew 5:28 KJV, "But I say unto you, That whosoever looketh on a woman to lust after her hath committed adultery with her already in his heart." What's in your heart? Who's in your heart? Before it's in the bed, it's in your heart. Just because you did not commit the physical act, does not mean that you did not commit adultery. Let Christ lead and rule your thoughts.

If you've committed adultery in your heart, or if you've committed the physical act, take this moment to repent and turn back to God. Physical or emotional adultery is a covenant-breaching offense to God and to your spouse. Choose to repent and turn back to Him.

## PRAYER

Father God, in the Name of Jesus, I repent of my sin. Father, I turn my life over to You. Father, I turn my heart over to You.

Father, forgive me of my sin. Father, wash me and make me white as snow.

Father, in the Name of Jesus, the Blood of Jesus Christ washes me and makes me whole. Lord, forgive me and make me new. Forgive me for breaking my Covenant with You and with my spouse. Lord, remove the taste of sin from my heart. Father, I choose to pursue You. Father, remove the stain of sin from our marriage.

Father, I surrender my heart to You. Father, I surrender my life to You. Lord, You are a Covenant-keeping God. Father, You are the Only Wise and True God. Father, there is no One like You. My heart safely trusts in You. My peace is found in You. Father, in You, there is safety. Father, I will put my trust in You forever.

Lord, lead my hands. Father, guide my heart. Lord, lead my feet. Father, guide my thoughts. Father, wash me. Lord, make me new.

Father, I surrender to Your Love. Father, I surrender to You — now and forever. Father, I am Yours. I receive the Blood of Your Son, Jesus Christ. I surrender every area of my life to You.

In Jesus' Name. Amen.

# Day 9

# A NEW CREATURE

*Therefore if any man be in Christ, he is a new creature: old things are passed away; behold, all things are become new.*

2 CORINTHIANS 5:17 KJV

When you accept Jesus Christ, as your Lord and Savior, you become new. When you are in Christ, you are a new creature. According to Strong's Concordance, the Greek word for Creature is *ktisis* (G2937), which means "The act of founding, establishing, building, the act of creating, creation, or anything created."

When you are in Christ, the sin of your old man is passed away. The sum of your old life, the misdeeds, and transgressions of the past are passed away. When you are in Christ, you become a new creature. Same skin, but a new heart.

According to Strong's Concordance, the Greek word *ktisis* (G2937) has another definition; Creature also means "The act of founding an institution or ordinance." Therefore, if any marriage is in Christ, it is a new creature. The institution of marriage was created by God. He established the institution for Himself. God created marriage to reflect His Love on Earth.

Ever since the beginning, Satan was after the institution of marriage, since the Garden of Eden. Satan wanted to separate husband and wife from the beginning of time. The enemy wanted to pervert hearts and taint marriages since the beginning. Satan wanted to separate mankind from God since the beginning.

When you surrender to Christ, not only do you become new, but everything under your stewardship becomes new. When your marriage submits to Christ, the borders, emotional boundaries, and the spiritual landscape become new. When a marriage is in Christ, it belongs to Him. And God gives you the authority and power to crush and to dominate anything that's not like Him.

Remember what God told Adam and Eve in the Garden of Eden? "And the Lord God commanded the man, saying, Of every tree of the garden thou mayest freely eat: But of the tree of the knowledge of good and evil, thou shalt not eat of it: for in the day that thou eatest thereof thou shalt surely die." Genesis 2:16–17 KJV. Adam and Eve could have eaten from all the trees of the garden, except for one. God outlined Adam and Eve's spiritual and physical boundaries.

Within the walls of your marriage, when God gives orders, choose to follow them. Let His Word shape the boundaries of your house. Obedience breeds blessing. Disobedience breeds curses and cycles. Submission to God's Word breeds blessing and breakthrough. Rejecting God's Word ignites seasons of withering and wilderness. Adam and Eve's disobedience ignited a cycle of wilderness for generations to come.

It's your choice. You can be the progenitor of establishing a generational blueprint of blessings or you can establish a pattern of generational cycles and curses. You choose. Set the pattern of life. Be the pattern of God's Light. When you are in Christ, you are a new creature, and the cycles of generations past are instantly broken.

When you are in Christ, you don't have to follow the patterns of past generations. The old ways of the world are destroyed, and you are new in Him. Surrender your heart to Him. Surrender your ways over to Him. Surrender your marriage over to Christ.

Ephesians 4:22 KJV declares, "That ye put off concerning the former conversation the old man, which is corrupt according to the deceitful lusts;" It's your choice to put off the old man. When you are in Christ, it is your choice to put on a new language — His Language. The former way of doing things has to die. The old language has to yield to God's Word and His Way of doing things. Your old man, your carnal past, must bow and submit to your new regenerated man in Christ.

When you are in Christ, you handle the heart of others in a new way. When you handle the heart of your spouse, you do it in a new way — His Way. When you are in Christ, the old way of doing things must flee and the new Way must flood in. Choose the new way — His Way. Choose the new heart. "A new heart also will I give you, and a new spirit will I put within you: and I will take away the stony heart out of your flesh, and I will give you an heart of flesh." Ezekiel 36:26 KJV.

## Day 10

# SIN CORRUPTS YOUR HARVEST

When sin enters your marriage, you taint the ground of your family. When sin entangles your heart, the generational lineage of your family suffers. Sin chokes and corrodes your family's bloodline. Sin taints the environment of your home. Sin eats away at and tears down the walls of your family.

Sin entangles the ground of your heart and holds your heart hostage. After Adam sinned, sin's impact had a lasting effect on Adam and the generations that followed after him. Adam's sin did not only impact him, but the consequence of his sin was felt by everything and everyone under his stewardship and authority.

The sin of one entangled the lives of many. Because of sin, Adam and his family spent generations in the wilderness toiling. Don't toil in the wilderness. Sin does not only impact you, it impacts everyone and everything attached to you. Sin wants to "reward" you with wilderness. Romans 6:23 KJV declares, "For the wages of sin is death; but the gift of God is eternal life through Jesus Christ our Lord." Don't wander in the wilderness. Adam forfeited his harvest and relinquished his authority because of his disobedience.

Sin separates. In Genesis 3:9–10 KJV, God called out to Adam, "Where Art thou?" Sin will cause you to abandon your post. Remember, God planted Adam in the Garden of Eden.

Adam's role was to tend to and to protect everything in the Garden of Eden. In fact, the Garden was only the starting point. In Genesis 1:26 KJV God declares, "Let us make man in our image, after our likeness: and let them have dominion over the fish of the sea, and over the fowl of the air, and over the cattle, and over all the earth, and over every creeping thing that creepeth upon the earth." Let them have dominion. Adam was the lord over the Garden but his domain was the world. Sin limits your dominion.

As long as Adam was submitted to God, the Lord of lords, God allowed him to lord over the land. What land has God called you to lord? What garden has God called you to have dominion over? What's your assignment? Adam disobeyed God and forfeited the Garden. Disobedience will lead you into the wilderness.

When Adam disobeyed God, he gave up his authority. Don't give up your authority. Adam was God's delegated authority on Earth. When man disobeyed God, his spiritual and natural authority was stripped. Sin strips you. Mankind needed a Savior to reconcile man back to God. Sin separates and obedience accelerates. Let God accelerate your destiny by surrendering to Him.

Your marriage is your God-given Garden. In order to appropriately lead and steward the Garden, you must follow His Word. Obey God in the Garden and He will give you the world. Don't despise small beginnings. Don't despise the small steps. Don't take for granted the small private victories in your house. With obedience comes enlargement.

Satan wants you to wither. The enemy wants you to abandon your post. Satan wants to derail you from fulfilling your assignment and walking in your purpose. God wanted Adam and Eve to have dominion over the entire world. Satan wanted Adam and Eve to be enslaved to him. Who will you serve? God or Satan? It's your choice. Obey God.

Sin corrupts generational legacy. Sin corrodes promise. Choose to serve God and fulfill the promise that God has set aside for you and your family. Satan is not just after you, he is after your seed. Satan wants what's coming out of you. Satan wants your physical seed and your spiritual seed. He wants to choke your harvest. The fruit that comes out of you, both naturally and spiritually, gives God glory, and Satan does not want anything or anyone to give God glory. Choose to let your life, your marriage, and everything produced by your hands reflect God and give Him Glory.

## Day 11

# FORGIVE FREELY

*Then came Peter to him, and said, Lord, how oft shall my brother sin against me, and I forgive him? till seven times? Jesus saith unto him, I say not unto thee, Until seven times: but, Until seventy times seven.*

MATTHEW 18:21-22 KJV

Forgive her. Forgive him. Your spouse is not your enemy. In Matthew 18:21–22 KJV, Peter asks Christ, "How many times shall I forgive someone who sins against me?" Christ replies, "And if he trespass against thee seven times in a day, and seven times in a day turn again to thee, saying, I repent; thou shalt forgive him." Luke 17:4 KJV expounds on the concept of forgiveness a little further. Christ responds to Peter by commanding him to forgive daily. Forgive frequently. Forgive often.

Think about it, if Christ commands us to forgive our brother or sister daily then how much more are we to forgive our spouse? Essentially, what Christ was commanding Peter was to keep a "heart posture" of forgiveness. Stay ready to forgive.

As Christians, we are to live a lifestyle of forgiveness. Christ freely forgave us so we should forgive others freely. Be willing and ready to forgive in all seasons. Psalms 86:5 KJV declares,

"For thou, Lord, art good, and ready to forgive; and plenteous in mercy unto all them that call upon thee." If God has forgiven us for our sins, then we are to extend the same forgiveness to others freely—including our spouse.

Choose to create an environment of forgiveness within the walls of your marriage. When you forgive, you create an environment of peace—God's Peace. When you forgive, you create an environment of freedom—God's Freedom. Don't hold on to the offense of the past. Release yourself and your marriage from the bondage of the past. Choose to forgive freely and frequently.

Luke 17:4 KJV outlines a pattern of forgiveness for your marriage, "And if he trespass against thee seven times in a day, and seven times in a day turn again to thee, saying, I repent; thou shalt forgive him." There is freedom in forgiving. Stay in a posture of forgiveness.

Think about it this way, when you forgive, it frees your heart from the weight of the past. When you rehearse the offense of the past, you relive the pain of the moment. Let the past go. Choose to forgive. When your heart is chained to the bondage of the past, it lords over you. Holding on to the weight of the past creates a bitter and hardened heart.

It's your choice to create an environment of peace or a place of bitterness within the heart of your marriage. Forgiveness heals hearts. Forgiveness heals marriages. Forgive her. Forgive him. Forgive each other freely.

## COUPLES' PRAYER

Father God, in the Name of Jesus, we thank You for our marriage. We thank You for Your Son, Jesus Christ. We thank You that through the shed Blood of Jesus Christ, we are forgiven. Through the shed Blood of Jesus Christ, we are free. Through Jesus Christ, we are set free from the bondage of the past and the entanglement of sin. Through the shed Blood of Jesus Christ, we are made new.

Father, let forgiveness rule within the heart of our marriage. Father, let our words reflect You. Father, our marriage is whole in You. Father, we surrender every aspect of our marriage, life, and family over to You.

Lord, we honor You. Father, this house surrenders to You. Father, You have forgiven us freely; therefore, we choose to forgive each other freely.

In Jesus' Name. Amen.

## ACTION

- Make a conscious effort to forgive daily.

- Decide not to blame each other for past sins, mistakes, failures, and shortcomings. Let the past go and choose to forgive frequently.

- Pray and ask God to soften your heart. Ask God for the "Faith to Forgive". It takes strength to forgive. You don't have the capacity to forgive in your own strength. Remember, it is God who gives you the strength to forgive.

- Surrender your heart and marriage over to God. Let the past go and move forward together.

## Day 12

# CORRUPT COMMUNICATION

*Let no corrupt communication proceed out of your mouth, but that which is good to the use of edifying, that it may minister grace unto the hearers.*

EPHESIANS 4:29 KJV

Communication is the key to cultivating the ground of your marriage. Good communication cultivates an environment of peace. Corrupt communication cultivates an environment of chaos and division within the heart of your marriage.

Choose your words wisely. When your words reflect the Heart of Christ, you'll create an environment of peace, power, purpose, and understanding. When your words reflect the Word of God, you'll establish a rich environment of peace and productivity. Choose to season your words with grace.

Are your words ministering to the heart of your spouse? Or are your words sowing seeds of discord? Proverbs 18:20 KJV declares, "A man's belly shall be satisfied with the fruit of his mouth; and with the increase of his lips shall he be filled." The fruit of your mouth, or your words, are seeds that are sown into the heart of your marriage. It's your choice to feed your marriage with words of life or you can poison the ground of your marriage with contaminated seed. Your words have power.

Ephesians 4:29 AMPC declares, "Let no foul or polluting language, nor evil word nor unwholesome or worthless talk [ever] come out of your mouth, but only such [speech] as is good and beneficial to the spiritual progress of others, as is fitting to the need and the occasion, that it may be a blessing and give grace (God's favor) to those who hear it." How you handle your spouse matters to God. Choose your words wisely. Choose to season your words with grace, both in private and in public.

When your spouse hears your words, let them minister and feed the heart of your spouse. Before you respond, choose to let God season your response with grace. James 1:19 KJV declares, "Wherefore, my beloved brethren, let every man be swift to hear, slow to speak, slow to wrath:" Choose to be swift to hear and careful to respond. Your response ministers to the heart of your spouse and feeds the ground of your marriage.

A corrupt response can contaminate the "communication arteries" of your marriage. Before you respond, choose to ask God for wisdom on how to handle the heart of your spouse. James 1:5 KJV declares, "If any of you lack wisdom, let him ask of God, that giveth to all men liberally, and upbraideth not; and it shall be given him." God gives wisdom liberally — just ask.

Before you respond, take some time and ask God how to respond to your spouse with wisdom. Ask God to lead your heart and to guide your words wisely. Your words can shipwreck a conversation or they can minister to your spouse. Let your words minister to the heart of the matter.

Proverbs 15:1 KJV declares, "A soft answer turneth away wrath: but grievous words stir up anger." Choose to apply this principle in Proverbs 15:1 KJV daily — a soft answer, or a mature and seasoned answer, turns away wrath. An answer that's regulated by God turns away wrath. Choose to pace yourself, and season your words with His Grace and allow God to lead the course of the conversation. Proverbs 15:1 NLT puts it this way, "A gentle answer deflects anger, but harsh words make tempers flare."

## Try working out these biblical principles and exercises before you begin a difficult discussion or conversation with your spouse

### ▸ Pray Privately

"But thou, when thou prayest, enter into thy closet, and when thou hast shut thy door, pray to thy Father which is in secret; and thy Father which seeth in secret shall reward thee openly." Matthew 6:6 KJV.

Pray and ask God to soften and lead your heart first. Let God handle your heart before you handle the heart of your spouse. A wounded heart cannot sow healing. It is difficult for an offended heart to hear the heart of their spouse. A hardened heart perverts the words that are both received and spoken. Ask God to heal your heart. Choose not to sow hurt or discord. Choose to be selfless and surrender to God. He will lead you and guide your conversation.

### ▸ Ask God for Wisdom

"If any of you lack wisdom, let him ask of God, that giveth to all men liberally, and upbraideth not; and it shall be given him." James 1:5 KJV.

God will give you Wisdom on how to handle difficult matters. Before you go to your spouse, ask God for Wisdom. Ask God for His Direction on what to say, when to say it, and even how to say it. Corrupt communication destroys marriages. Let God fill you with His Wisdom.

### ▸ The Posture of Peace

"And let the peace of God rule in your hearts, to the which also ye are called in one body; and be ye thankful." Colossians 3:15 KJV.

Let the Peace of God rule your thoughts. Don't focus on the offense. Focus on God. Before you go to your spouse, surrender your heart to the God of Peace. 1 Peter 5:7 KJV declares, "Casting all your care upon him; for he careth for you." When you cast your cares to God, you release your heart from the bondage and the grip of the offense. Grab His Peace and surrender the offense to Him. Let God posture your heart in a position of peace. "Blessed are the peacemakers: for they shall be called the children of God." Matthew 5:9 KJV.

Notice that the principles listed above all deal with your heart first. God handles your heart before He handles the heart of others. It starts with you. Submit your flesh to God and let Christ lead your actions.

### ▸ Ask Your Spouse

"To every thing there is a season, and a time to every purpose under the heaven:" Ecclesiastes 3:1 KJV.

Everything has a specific time and purpose. Every conversation has a proper time and purpose. Ask your spouse if this is the appropriate time to have a conversation. Set the heart of your spouse. Set the environment of the conversation. Let the Peace of God lead you. Let His Peace rule the tone of the conversation. If now is not a good time then come together to set an appropriate time in the near future. Season your words and respond with grace.

### ▸ Get an Understanding

"Wisdom is the principal thing; therefore get wisdom: and with all thy getting get understanding." Proverbs 4:7 KJV.

The purpose of the conversation is to get an understanding — not to blame but to get an understanding. Let God fill your heart with wisdom on how to receive and how to respond. Let your heart be softened and ripe to receive your spouse's words in order to get an understanding. Let your words be filled with His Love and Grace. Position the conversation, from the beginning, to get an understanding. Before you speak, choose to engage God and pray together. Pray for wisdom, pray that God leads and softens your heart, pray for clarity, insight, and direction. Let God fill the ground of your home with wisdom and witty ways to handle the heart of your spouse.

### ▸ Handle Your Spouse According to Knowledge

"Likewise, ye husbands, dwell with them according to knowledge, giving honour unto the wife, as unto the weaker vessel, and as being heirs together of the grace of life; that your prayers be not hindered." 1 Peter 3:7 KJV.

Handle your spouse according to your intimate knowledge of them. Handle your spouse according to the information and wisdom that God has given to you about them. Through prayer, God will give you wisdom on how to handle the heart of your spouse.

### ▸ As They Went

"And as he entered into a certain village, there met him ten men that were lepers, which stood afar off: And they lifted up their voices, and said, Jesus, Master, have mercy on us. And when he saw them, he said unto them, Go shew yourselves unto the priests. And it came to pass, that, as they went, they were cleansed." Luke 17:12-14 KJV.

A leper, in biblical times, were people who were considered "unclean" because of their outward skin condition. No one wanted to touch or be around lepers. Notice, in Luke 17:12 KJV, the lepers were standing afar off. Maybe, this conversation is like the lepers—no one wants to discuss the sensitive matter. It is "afar off" and is considered as a "sticking point" or a point of contention in your marriage. Notice what the lepers declared to Jesus in Luke 17:13 KJV, "Have mercy on us." Have mercy on your spouse. Let the environment of your conversation be filled with mercy. Healing takes place after mercy is released. Let your "leprous conversation" be healed as you present the "fleshy matter" to God. As you present your conversation to God, you'll be healed. Do these exercises continually and you'll mature in how to communicate difficult or leprous conversations.

### ▸ Cast Your Care Together

"Casting the whole of your care [all your anxieties, all your worries, all your concerns, once and for all] on Him, for He cares for you affectionately and cares about you watchfully." 1 Peter 5:7 AMPC.

Choose to cast your cares together. Don't "cast" alone. Remember, the enemy wants to divide you through isolation. Cast together. Pray together. Love together. Forgive together. Heal together. Mature together. Grow together.

Your spouse is not the enemy. If tempers begin to flare, step back, take a moment to recalibrate, pray, and ask God to soften your heart. Focus on your response. Meditate on your response. Season your words with grace. Pray and ask God for wisdom and understanding. Ask God to navigate your heart and to lead the conversation and go back to Step 1. Communication is an art, and remember, your spouse is not the enemy. Effective communication is a muscle that needs to be exercised and matured consistently.

Corrupt communication corrupts hearts. Bitter communication contaminates hearts. Hurt people hurt others. At the core of anger is an offense and behind every offense is a hurt or wound. Hurt people hurt others. Wounded people wound others. Are you wounded? Before you respond, out of hurt, ask God to heal your heart. Before you respond, out of offense, ask God to lead your heart. Your contaminated words can create a hostile and polluted environment. Let God heal you. Let God heal your marriage. Let His Word lead and heal your family.

## ACTION

- Choose to season your words with grace. Decide not to pollute the ground of your marriage with corrupt words.

- Choose to forgive freely. Don't blame each other for past sins, mistakes, failures, and shortcomings. Let the past go and choose to season your response with grace.

- Pray and ask God to soften your heart. Ask God to guide your speech. Ask God to lead your words before you respond.

- Surrender your heart, marriage, and response over to God. Let the past go and move forward together. Let the offense go and move forward in peace, grace, love, respect, and honor.

# COUPLES' PRAYER

Father God, in the Name of Jesus, we thank You for our marriage. We thank You that Your Word guides and leads our hearts. Father, we thank You that our marriage is filled with Your Love and Grace.

Father, we thank You that our marriage is covered by You. Father, we ask that You shower our home with Your Wisdom. Fill our conversation with Your Grace and Love. Let our conversation reflect You in public and in private.

Father, heal every area of our marriage. Father, heal us from past wounds. Father, grant us the Grace to forgive. Lord, lead us. Guide our footsteps. Lead our conversation.

Father, let us grow together. Father, let us love together. Father, let us forgive together. Father, lead our thoughts. Lord, wash our hearts with Your Love in every area of our lives.

In Jesus' Name. Amen.

## Day 13

## LEAD HER IN LOVE

*For the husband is the head of the wife,
even as Christ is the head of the church:
and he is the saviour of the body.*

EPHESIANS 5:23 KJV

God has set the husband as the head of the family, not as a means of control but as a means to serve. The husband is not a dictator. The husband is not a ruling oppressive master. Oppression is not love. God has set the husband over the family in order to cover, protect, provide, and serve as a reflection of His Character and Love.

Leadership is not control. As the husband, you can lead her without controlling her heart. Lead her gracefully. God has given you the power to lead her by reflecting the Love of Christ. Let God display His Love through your deeds, words, and actions. Choose to be selfless. Crucify selfish behavior and lead through service. Lead her through your submission to Christ. Let your love reflect the Love and the Heart of Christ.

As the husband, there are certain things that God holds you responsible for. The husband is accountable directly to God for the spiritual governance, oversight, and execution of the garden — your home. Notice what Genesis 3:9 KJV declares, "And the Lord God called unto Adam, and said unto him, Where art thou?" God was looking for Adam. God called for Adam. God was searching for His leader — Adam. God assigned Adam to a particular place and he was not there. Adam was absent. Leadership is weighty — husbands report their affairs to God.

Husband, as the spiritual covering of the family and head of the home, you are to steward and protect the gifts that God has given you — your family. Remember Adam's assignment in Genesis? "The Lord God placed the man in the Garden of Eden to tend and watch over it." Genesis 2:15 NLT. Your responsibility is to tend to and to watch over what God has given you — your family. Your family is your garden. Everything that's attached to your family and home is assigned to your stewardship. Be fruitful and multiply.

Genesis 3:8-9 NLT declares, "When the cool evening breezes were blowing, the man and his wife heard the Lord God walking about in the garden. So they hid from the Lord God among the trees. Then the Lord God called to the man, "Where are you?" Notice, in Genesis 3:8, God called to the man, "Where are you?" God was looking for Adam. Although Adam and Eve sinned together, God set Adam as the head to lead, direct, and protect the house from engaging in sin. God gave Adam the spiritual and natural charge to tend to the Garden and to proactively watch over it.

Adam, your responsibility is to lead her in wisdom, and in love, by obeying God's Word. Passivity is not an option. You are responsible for the advancement and the productivity of your home. Their education, both spiritual and natural, is under your stewardship. Their spiritual and natural development is under your stewardship. The financial productivity and stability of the house are under your stewardship. Choose to be active, be submitted to God, and be present.

An absent husband, or father, is no excuse. Adam, when he sinned, abandoned his post. Disobedience will cause you to abandon your assignment. When Adam sinned, he created a generational cycle of absenteeism and passivity that still plagues mankind today. Choose to be present. Choose to be active. Choose to be a present and active husband. Choose to be a present and active father. Choose to be a present and active leader.

When you willfully disobey God's command for your house, you're establishing a generational pattern of disobedience, perversion, and rebellion. When you disobey God, you're setting your house up for generational failure. Disobedience breeds wilderness.

Adam's disobedience sent a shockwave through the Earth. Adam's sin caused generations to stay stuck in a stagnant cycle of sin and lack. Your seemingly small act of sin committed today has cyclical consequences for generations to come. But thanks be unto God, through Jesus Christ, we do not have to succumb to the prison sentence of sin through Adam. Although Adam sinned, we have assurance through Jesus Christ that we can be set free from the stronghold of sin. Christ breaks cycles. Jesus Christ broke every generational cycle. Christ conquered the wilderness.

Romans 5:19 AMPC declares, "For just as by one man's disobedience (failing to hear, heedlessness, and carelessness) the many were constituted sinners, so by one Man's obedience the many will be constituted righteous (made acceptable to God, brought into right standing with Him)."

It's your choice to submit to God and lead your wife as God leads your heart and actions. Or you can submit to the entanglement of sin and perpetuate a generational cycle of sin, bondage, bitterness, entanglement, rage, and poverty. Lead her in love.

Lead her as God leads your heart. Lead her in wisdom. If you lack wisdom, as to how to lead her, surround yourself with wise, God-given, mature, and seasoned counselors.

1 Peter 3:7 KJV declares, "Likewise, ye husbands, dwell with them according to knowledge, giving honour unto the wife, as unto the weaker vessel, and as being heirs together of the grace of life; that your prayers be not hindered." Study her. Love her. Learn her. Lead her according to your intimate knowledge of her.

If you don't know how to lead her, simply ask God. He created her. Remember, she was God's daughter before she was your wife. He created every part of her and knew her intimately before the foundations of the world. Jeremiah 1:5 KJV declares, "Before I formed thee in the belly I knew thee; and before thou camest forth out of the womb I sanctified thee, and I ordained thee a prophet unto the nations."

Before your wife was formed in her mother's womb — God knew her. God handcrafted her. God knows every intimate part of her. He knows her emotional capacity. He knows her intellectual capabilities and strengths. He knows her. He is intimately aware of her talents and abilities — He placed them in her, so why not ask Him how to skillfully lead her?

Ask God for the wisdom to lead. James 1:5 KJV declares, "If any of you lack wisdom, let him ask of God, that giveth to all men liberally, and upbraideth not; and it shall be given him." God gives wisdom liberally. He gives wisdom for marriage. He gives wisdom for any area of your life. He gives wisdom for leading in business. He gives wisdom for leading in ministry. He gives wisdom for leading in government. He gives wisdom for leading your family. He gives wisdom for anything that you ask for.

Wisdom is the foundation of your life. Just ask Him. Wisdom is the foundation and the bedrock of your marriage. "Wisdom is the principal thing; therefore get wisdom: and with all thy getting get understanding." Proverbs 4:7 KJV. Get an understanding of how to lead her in every season. Seasons change, and as you grow, the style, strength, and temperament of your leadership will change. Let God transform and lead your heart. Let God lead your marriage as you submit to God. Lead her selflessly. Love is selfless. Love reflects the Heart of Christ. Submit to God and let your actions reflect His Heart, Love, and Character—in every season of life.

## ACTION

- Choose to season your words with grace. Ask God for the grace to lead your family. Ask God for the wisdom to lead them in every season.

- Decide not to pollute the ground of your marriage with corrupt words and actions.

- Ask God to soften your heart. Choose to surrender to God even when it's difficult.

- Ask God to guide your speech. Ask God to lead your words before you respond.

- Surrender your heart and every area of your marriage over to God.

# A HUSBAND'S PRAYER

Father God, in the Name of Jesus, I thank You for my wife. Father, I thank You that You made her in Your image. I thank You for my marriage.

Father, I thank You for softening my heart. Father, I thank You for guiding the heart of our marriage. Lord, lead me. Father, guide my tongue in every season. Father, grant me the grace to be an example of Your Love and Character.

Father, I choose to surrender to You in every season of my life. Father, I choose to trust You. Lord, guide my footsteps. Lord, forgive me of my trespasses. Lord, order my steps. Father, I surrender my heart to You. Father, I surrender my life to You. Father, in the Name of Jesus, I surrender my marriage over to You. Father, lead me. I surrender to You.

In Jesus' Name. Amen.

## Day 14

# THE DEEP WELLS OF COMMUNICATION

*The words of a man's mouth are as deep waters, and the wellspring of wisdom as a flowing brook.*

PROVERBS 18:4 KJV

Communication serves as the wellspring of your heart. Your words, and word selection, are vital arteries that feed every aspect of your life, family, and marriage. They (your words) aide to the health, longevity, and consistent maturation of your heart and establishes the foundation and framework of your marriage. Your words are vital.

May every aspect of your communication reflect the Heart, Character, Wisdom, and Counsel of God. May your words be a wellspring of life and overflow with Grace and Wisdom. May your words minister to and feed the heart of your family and marriage.

Proverbs 3:8 KJV puts it this way, "It shall be health to thy navel, and marrow to thy bones." May your words be health to the heart of your marriage. "This will bring health to your body and nourishment to your bones." Proverbs 3:8 NIV.

As you surrender every word to God, and trust in His Way of doing things, He will lead and guide your path. Before you speak, choose to submit your words to Christ. Surrender every aspect of your language to Christ. "Then you will have healing for your body and strength for your bones." Proverbs 3:8 NLT.

There is healing in your grace-filled words. For Psalm 147:3 KJV declares, "He healeth the broken in heart, and bindeth up their wounds." When your words are seasoned with His Grace and Wisdom Proverbs 16:24 NLT declares, "Kind words are like honey—sweet to the soul and healthy for the body." Wise, grace-filled words are sweet to the soul of your marriage and heals deep wounds of the past.

The Amplified Version expounds upon Proverbs 16:24 AMPC in the following manner, "Pleasant words are as a honeycomb, sweet to the mind and healing to the body." Pleasant words are sweet to the mind. When you sow pleasant words, you'll create a culture of peace within the heart of your family and marriage.

Philippians 4:8 KJV expounds upon communication in the following manner, "Finally, brethren, whatsoever things are true, whatsoever things are honest, whatsoever things are just, whatsoever things are pure, whatsoever things are lovely, whatsoever things are of good report; if there be any virtue, and if there be any praise, think on these things." Think on these things.

The Amplified Version expounds upon Proverbs 15:1 AMPC in the following manner, "A SOFT answer turns away wrath, but grievous words stir up anger." A soft answer heals. A soft and grace-filled response can heal old wounds and pluck up offensive bitter seeds of the past. Let your words minister to the heart of your spouse.

Ephesians 4:29 KJV declares, "Let no corrupt communication proceed out of your mouth, but that which is good to the use of edifying, that it may minister grace unto the hearers."

Minister Wisdom, Grace, and Peace to the heart of your marriage and your spouse.

The Amplified Version expounds upon Psalm 49:3 AMPC in the following manner, "My mouth shall speak wisdom; and the meditation of my heart shall be understanding." Let your mouth speak the Wisdom of God and let your heart surrender to His Understanding. Let the infallible Word of God shape the infrastructure of your daily conduct, character, and conversation.

The Amplified Version expounds upon Proverbs 10:14 AMPC in the following manner, "Wise men store up knowledge [in mind and heart], but the mouth of the foolish is a present destruction." Speak words of Wisdom instead of sowing seeds of discord. For the mouth of the foolish spews destruction.

The New International Version expounds upon Proverbs 10:14 NIV in the following manner, "The wise store up knowledge, but the mouth of a fool invites ruin." The foolish invites ruin. Choose to sow Wisdom instead of heeding to the counsel of the foolish. For the heart and mouth of the wise is a deep springwell of Wisdom, Grace, and Peace.

Proverbs 15:7 NLT declares, "The lips of the wise give good advice; the heart of a fool has none to give." Follow the advice of the wise and run far from the counsel of the ungodly. For Proverbs 6:23 KJV declares, "The heart of the wise teacheth his mouth, and addeth learning to his lips."

Train your mouth to hold your peace and in all thy getting get understanding. For the way of the wise are as deep waters, and the wellspring of wisdom as a constant flowing brook. "Wisdom is the principal thing; therefore get wisdom: and with all thy getting get understanding." Proverbs 4:7 KJV

# A HUSBAND'S PRAYER

Father God, in the Name of Jesus, I thank You for my wife. Father, I thank You that she is a wellspring of life. Father, I thank You that she reflects Your Heart and Character. Father, I thank You that she is full of Wisdom and Counsel.

Father, may my words minister to and feed the heart of my wife. Father, may my words and actions build her up and not tear her down. May the words that flow from my mouth strengthen and develop our marriage.

Lord, let my words feed the core of our marriage. May my words sow life into the heart of my home and serve as constant nourishment to my family.

Father, I choose to submit my words to You before I speak. You are Lord and I surrender every aspect of my language over to You. Lord guide every word. Father, I trust in Your Way of doing things. For there is healing in Your Way of handling her heart.

Father, let my words satisfy her all the days of my life. Lord, let the words that flow from my mouth, lead and heal her heart. Father, let my words Glorify You and feed the heart of our home. For You Lord, heal broken hearts and bind up old wounds.

Lord, season my words with Grace and Wisdom. Father, let my words be sweet and honey to her soul. Father, lead my response and guide my words. Lord, in times of turmoil, teach me how to give a soft response.

Father, let my grace-filled words heal old wounds and pluck up offensive bitter seeds of the past. Father, let my words minister to the heart of my marriage.

In Jesus' Name. Amen.

# A WIFE'S PRAYER

Father God, in the Name of Jesus, I thank You for my husband. Father, I thank You that he reflects Your Heart and Character. Father, I thank You that he is full of Wisdom and Counsel. Father, I thank You that he is a deep wellspring of life.

Father, may my words minister to and feed the heart of my husband. Father, may my words and actions build him up and not tear him down. May the words that flow from my mouth strengthen and develop our marriage.

Lord, let my words feed the core of our marriage. May my words sow life into the heart of my home and serve as constant nourishment to my family.

Father, I choose to submit my words to You before I speak. You are Lord and I surrender every aspect of my language over to You. Lord guide every word. Father, I trust in Your Way of doing things. For there is healing in Your Way of handling the heart of my husband.

Father, let my words satisfy him all the days of my life. Lord, let the words that flow from my mouth, feed and heal his heart. Father, let my words Glorify You and feed the heart of our home. For You Lord, heal broken hearts and bind up old wounds.

Lord, season my words with Grace and Wisdom. Father, let my words be sweet and honey to his soul. Father, lead my response and guide my words. Lord, in times of turmoil, teach me how to give a soft response.

Father, let my grace-filled words heal old wounds and pluck up offensive bitter seeds of the past. Father, let my words minister to the heart of my marriage.

In Jesus' Name. Amen.

# A COUPLES' PRAYER

Father God, in the Name of Jesus, we thank You for our marriage. Father, we thank You that our marriage reflects Your Heart and Character. Father, we thank You that we are full of Wisdom and Counsel. Father, we thank You that we are a wellspring of life.

Father, may our words minister to and feed the heart of our marriage. Father, may our words and actions build up and not tear down. May the words that flow from our mouths strengthen and develop the infrastructure of our marriage.

Lord, let our words feed the core of our marriage. May our words sow life and health into the heart of our home and nourish our bodies.

Father, we choose to submit our words to You before we speak. You are Lord and we surrender every aspect of our language over to You. Lord guide every word. Father, we trust in Your Way of doing things. For there is healing in Your Way of handling our hearts.

Father, let our words satisfy each other all the days of our lives. Lord, let the words that flow from our mouth, heal the heart of our marriage. Father, let our words Glorify You and feed the heart of our home. For You Lord, heal broken hearts and bind up old wounds.

Lord, season our words with Grace and Wisdom. Father, let our words be sweet and honey to our soul. Father, lead our response and guide our words. Lord, in times of turmoil, teach us how to give a soft response.

Father, let our grace-filled words heal old wounds and pluck up offensive bitter seeds of the past. Father, let our words minister to the heart of our marriage.

In Jesus' Name. Amen.

## Day 15

# SUBMISSION IS NOT BONDAGE... IT'S POWER

*Submitting yourselves one to another in the fear of God.*

EPHESIANS 5:21 KJV

Submission is not bondage, nor is submission a prison sentence. Submission is powerful. Submission is liberating. A couple submitted to God is a powerful force to be reckoned with. In fact, the more you choose to submit to God as a couple, and to each other, the more God will exalt you.

Matthew 23:12 KJV declares, "And whosoever shall exalt himself shall be abased; and he that shall humble himself shall be exalted." Can God trust you with more? Can He trust you with more influence? Can He trust you with more authority? Can God trust you to steward over more resources? Before God enlarges you, He examines your heart. God examines your ability to submit. Submit to Him.

Submission requires humility. Submission requires discipline. In fact, submission is an art. Submission is the foundation of leadership. Great leaders submit to authority. Anything that's built for the long term must have a strong foundation and infrastructure.

In order to build a great marriage, love and submission must be its foundation. Without love and submission, marriages implode. Pride kills marriages. Pride destroys families. Pride ruins legacies. Pride is the enemy of submission. Proverbs 16:18 KJV declares, "Pride goeth before destruction, and an haughty spirit before a fall."

When you see pride raise its ugly head, know that destruction is near. Prideful actions lead to a haughty heart. A haughty spirit leads to a fall. Whenever you feel pride raising its head, choose to abase yourself. Choose to humble yourself. Choose to surrender to God in the moments of heated discussion.

Pride is deceitful and will corrupt the foundation of your marriage. Submission is powerful. When you submit to the Word of God, God declares that He will exalt you in due time. 1 Peter 5:6 KJV states, "Humble yourselves therefore under the mighty hand of God, that he may exalt you in due time:"

According to Strong's Concordance, the Greek word for Submit is *hypotassō* (G5293), which means "To arrange under, to subordinate, to subject, put in subjection, to subject one's self, obey, to submit to one's control, to yield to one's admonition or advice, to obey, or to be subject." Submit yourselves to the Word of God. When you "arrange under" the Word of God, He will lead and guide the heart of your marriage. When you subject yourself to the Word of God and yield to His Advice and Counsel, you will have good success.

Notice what Joshua 1:8 KJV declares, "This book of the law shall not depart out of thy mouth; but thou shalt meditate therein day and night, that thou mayest observe to do according to all that is written therein: for then thou shalt make thy way prosperous, and then thou shalt have good success." If you submit to the Word of God, and "arrange yourself" under its instruction, both day and night, you will have good success — this includes your marriage.

Notice what Deuteronomy 28:1 KJV declares, "And it shall come to pass, if thou shalt hearken diligently unto the voice of the Lord thy God, to observe and to do all his commandments which I command thee this day, that the Lord thy God will set thee on high above all nations of the earth." When you diligently submit to the Word of God, He will set you high above all the nations of the Earth.

Submission is powerful. Submission is not weakness. Well, in a sense, submission is a form of weakness. Paul declares this principle best in 2 Corinthians 12:9–10 KJV, "And he said unto me, My grace is sufficient for thee: for my strength is made perfect in weakness. Most gladly therefore will I rather glory in my infirmities, that the power of Christ may rest upon me. Therefore I take pleasure in infirmities, in reproaches, in necessities, in persecutions, in distresses for Christ's sake: for when I am weak, then am I strong." God's Grace is sufficient. God's strength is made perfect in your submission.

The New Living Translation expounds upon 2 Corinthians 12:9 NLT in the following manner, "My grace is all you need. My power works best in weakness." Let God's Power flow through you. Let His Power work through your marriage. Let His Power work through your language and conversation. Submit your marriage to God's Way of doing things.

Zechariah 4:6 KJV declares, "Then he answered and spake unto me, saying, This is the word of the Lord unto Zerubbabel, saying, Not by might, nor by power, but by my spirit, saith the Lord of hosts." This is the Word of the Lord to you, it's not by might, not by your own power, but by His Spirit that your marriage will prosper. Submission is powerful. Submit to God first. Build your marriage by submitting to God. Build your foundation on His Word. Let your covenant be centered on Christ. Submit to Christ.

Submit to the Cross. When you study out the physical composition of the Cross, it was two pieces of wood held together by a stake or nail bound together in a perpendicular form. One piece of the wood would be placed in the ground and positioned in an upright vertical fashion and the other would be placed across it in a horizontal form.

When the Romans placed their victims on the Cross, they would stretch the person's arms across the horizontal portion of the Cross and nail their hands to it. Then the Romans would take the person's body and stake it to the vertical piece of wood. The person nailed to the Cross would literally be hanging across it by their own weight.

With every move, the person would make, while on the Cross, the person would feel the nails that were driven in their hands. Additionally, as their arms were stretched out, their chest cavity would literally cave in, suffocating them as they tried to breathe. The person on the Cross would drown in their own blood as their chest cavity was being crushed by their own weight.

Notice the final Words of Christ, in John 19:30 KJV, "When Jesus therefore had received the vinegar, he said, It is finished: and he bowed his head, and gave up the ghost." Christ submitted to the Cross for you. Christ submitted to the Cross for your marriage. His arms were stretched wide in order to receive you. Choose to surrender your marriage to Christ.

The horizontal positioning of the Cross also represents the Earthly relationship between God and man. Christ died for you and your marriage. He died for you so that you can live. John 10:10 KJV declares, "The thief cometh not, but for to steal, and to kill, and to destroy: I am come that they might have life, and that they might have it more abundantly." Yes, Christ died for your sin — Christ also died so that you can live a fruitful, full, abundant, and satisfying life here on Earth.

Christ cares about your horizontal Earthly relationships. He cares about the health and wholeness of your family and your marriage. Jesus Christ stayed on that Cross for you. He had the Power to get up from the Cross but He chose to submit — for you. He was selfless. Submission is selfless. John 10:11 KJV declares, "I am the good shepherd: the good shepherd giveth his life for the sheep." As the True Shepherd, Christ gave Himself for His flock. Your family is your flock. Submission is powerful. Submission submits under a greater authority, a greater assignment, a greater purpose.

Submission carries weight. The weight of the Cross was excruciating. Sometimes, as a form of torment, the Romans had the victim carry their own Cross to the place where they were being crucified. Christ submitted His flesh to the crucifixion process for you. Christ carried the Cross for you. If Christ carried the Cross for you and your marriage — surely you can crucify your "flesh" in an emotional sense.

Submit and crucify your emotions by not speaking recklessly. Choose to crucify your flesh. Choose to selflessly do what God commands you to do within the walls of your marriage. Choose to selflessly love your spouse.

Christ was bound to the Cross by choice. His submission was not by force — Christ was bound by Love. Love is the foundation of submission. Love is what drove Christ to stay on the Cross until His flesh died. He laid down His life for you. Crucify and kill your flesh through Love.

Receive the work that Christ did on the Cross. Kill your fleshly desires. Crucify corrupt communication and kill your selfish ways. Christ died so that you can have the power to submit in His Strength. Submit to His Blood. Submit to His Strength. Submit to His Love.

Christ died for your sins. He died so that our Covenant with God the Father can be reconciled. Christ died for our vertical relationship with God. "For God so loved the world, that he gave his only begotten Son, that whosoever believeth in him should not perish, but have everlasting life." John 3:16 KJV. Remember the Cross. Every time pride tries to rear its ugly head within the borders of your marriage, choose to remember what Christ did on the Cross.

Isaiah 53:7 AMPC declares, "He was oppressed, [yet when] He was afflicted, He was submissive and opened not His mouth; like a lamb that is led to the slaughter, and as a sheep before her shearers is dumb, so He opened not His mouth." Christ was silent. While His flesh was being ripped from His body, He remained selfless. Christ is our example. Choose to crucify your flesh and submit your marriage to Christ. Let your marriage reflect and point to the Cross. Let your actions point to the Cross. Choose to remember the Cross.

Christ not only endured the Cross — He conquered it. Christ humbled himself and submitted to the Will of the Father. Philippians 2:8–9 KJV declares, "And being found in fashion as a man, he humbled himself, and became obedient unto death, even the death of the Cross. Wherefore God also hath highly exalted him, and given him a name which is above every name:" When you crush your flesh — exaltation comes. Promotion, expansion, and enlargement come after submission.

Let Christ be exalted within the confines of your marriage. Choose to surrender your words, thoughts, deeds, and actions to Him. Surrender to Christ and to each other. Do you want to be right? Or do you want your marriage? Don't let pride lead your marriage. Don't let bitterness corrode your heart. Choose to forgive. Choose to move forward.

## Day 16

# SUBMISSION IS A CHOICE

*Wives, submit yourselves unto your own husbands, as unto the Lord.*

EPHESIANS 5:22 KJV

Wives, you were God's daughter before you were a wife. God created and crafted you as His Own Treasure and Delight. Even before the foundations of the world, He knew you. Jeremiah 1:5 KJV declares, "Before I formed thee in the belly I knew thee; and before thou camest forth out of the womb I sanctified thee, and I ordained thee a prophet unto the nations."

According to Strong's Concordance, the Hebrew word for form is *yatsar* (H3335), which means "To fashion or frame." God fashioned and framed you to reflect His Glory and Honor on the Earth. Proverbs 12:4 KJV declares, "A virtuous woman is a crown to her husband: but she that maketh ashamed is as rottenness in his bones." You were created as virtue personified. A wife that's submitted to God reflects His Glory and Character on the Earth. In fact, a wife submitted to God brings Glory to the marriage.

Submission brings glory. Proverbs 12:4 AMPC declares, "A virtuous and worthy wife [earnest and strong in character] is a crowning joy to her husband, but she who makes him ashamed is as rottenness in his bones." A wife is a gift from God. Proverbs 19:14 KJV declares, "House and riches are the inheritance of fathers: and a prudent wife is from the Lord." God gives prudent wives to submitted kings. Proverbs 19:14 AMPC declares, "House and riches are the inheritance from fathers, but a wise, understanding, and prudent wife is from the Lord." Wisdom comes from God. According to Proverbs 19:14 AMPC, houses and riches are the inheritance from fathers. Understanding comes from God. Prudence comes from God. A prudent wife comes from the Lord.

God has packaged you with wisdom and understanding. A submitted daughter matures into a submitted queen. God calls you His Own and He will not lead you astray. With submission comes power and authority. Let's examine the power of submission in the New Testament with the story of the Centurion.

Matthew 8:9–10 KJV declares, "For I am a man under authority, having soldiers under me: and I say to this man, Go, and he goeth; and to another, Come, and he cometh; and to my servant, Do this, and he doeth it. When Jesus heard it, he marvelled, and said to them that followed, Verily I say unto you, I have not found so great faith, no, not in Israel."

Notice what the Centurion declares to Christ, "For I am a man under authority." The Centurion was a man of authority and yet he submitted. The Centurion submitted to those above him in his Roman rank. Christ was God in the flesh and yet Christ was submitted. He submitted to God the Father. You are a woman in authority, crafted by the Hand of God, before the foundations of the Earth; choose to submit. Yield to God.

Remember the Cross? The Cross had two parts: a horizontal and a vertical component. Submission has two parts: a vertical and a horizontal component. The vertical component of the Cross represents your spiritual submission to God. Notice that the Cross is planted in the ground. Spiritual submission starts on the ground. Before exaltation is given, before virtue is bestowed, before expansion occurs, submission starts on the ground—your prayer life. Your prayer life and your communication with God are a direct correlation with your spiritual growth and maturity.

Submission is for everyone. Ephesians 5:21 KJV declares, "Submitting yourselves one to another in the fear of God." A submitted marriage is a powerful marriage. Notice the second part of the Cross—the horizontal component. A marriage that's submitted to God and to each other is a unified powerhouse that will wreck the kingdom of darkness. That's why the enemy attacked the covenant of marriage from the beginning and continues to attack marriages to this day. The covenant of marriage points to the Cross. Marriage reflects the Cross. The vertical represents your submission to God and the horizontal represents your submission with man (your spouse). In marriage, the flesh is nailed to the Cross daily.

In marriage, pride dies and submission is exalted. Submission is a choice and brings about power. A powerless marriage is a defenseless marriage. Choose to submit to God's Word. Submission is power.

Deuteronomy 32:30 KJV declares, "How should one chase a thousand, and two put ten thousand to flight, except their Rock had sold them, and the Lord had shut them up?" Submission is a unified choice. Fight together and not against each other. Your spouse is not the enemy. You are a weapon against the enemy. A unified marriage is a powerful weapon against Satan and the kingdom of darkness. Deploy your weapon. War against the enemy and not against each other.

## PRAY FOR HIM

Father God, in the Name of Jesus, I thank You for my husband. I thank You for his leadership. I thank You for his wisdom. I thank You for his heart. Father, I thank You that his character reflects You.

Father, cover my husband. Father, bless the work of his hands. Father, bless him indeed and enlarge his territory, oversight, and responsibility.

Lord, lead him like David and order his steps. Father, lead him and give him unparalleled wisdom like Solomon. Father, I thank You for his life. Father, I thank You for everything that You've called him to be. Father, I thank You that he leads Your house in integrity. Father, guide his feet. Father, lead his heart. Father, let this house reflect Your Character.

Father, I am Your daughter and we surrender to You. We submit every area of our marriage to You.

In Jesus' Name. Amen.

## PRAY FOR HER

Father God, in the Name of Jesus, I thank You for my wife. I thank You for her wisdom, leadership, and character. I thank You for her heart. Father, I thank You that her character reflects You.

Father, cover our house. Father, cover my wife with favor and bless the work of her hands. Father, bless the fruit of her womb. Bless her indeed and enlarge her territory like never before.

Father, lead her like Esther and order her steps with kings. Let her find favor with every person that looks upon her. Father, lead her and give her witty ideas and unparalleled wisdom like this generation has never seen or heard before.

Let her character be known throughout this nation. Let her virtue be known throughout this generation. Let her children call her Blessed. Father, I call her Blessed. Father, You have called her Blessed.

Lord, I thank You for her life. I thank You for everything that you've called her to be. Father, I thank You that she leads and serves in integrity. Father, I thank You that she is a beacon of Glory for the world to see Your greatness through her. She is an example for generations to pattern and follow after.

Peace consumes her. Favor surrounds her. Joy overtakes her. Wisdom guides her. Integrity shields her. Father, lead her heart. Let our house reflect Your Peace, Glory, and Character. Father, I am Your son and this house surrenders to You — forever.

In Jesus' Name. Amen.

## PRAY TOGETHER

Father God, in the Name of Jesus, we thank You for our marriage. Father, we thank You for leading our home. Father, through Your Son, Jesus Christ, every generational bondage is broken.

Father, we thank You for showering our house with Wisdom. We thank You for the heart of our marriage. Father, we declare, in the Name of Jesus, that our marriage is good ground for You to dwell here.

Lord, dwell here. Father, we thank You that the character of this house reflects Your Heart. Father, cover us. Lord, lead us.

Father, we surrender to You. Father God, in the Name of Jesus, we submit to Your Way of doing things, both in private and in public.

Father, bless us indeed and enlarge our territory. Bless our house as we go in and go out in business. Father, let Your Favor consume us. Father, bless the work of our hands. Father, lead our family. Order our steps. Cover us.

Father, lead us and give us unparalleled wisdom like Solomon. Father, we thank You for our family. Father, we thank You for everything that You've called us to be.

Father, we thank You that we are a house that serves and leads in integrity. Father, guide our feet. Father, lead and soften our hearts. Let this house reflect Your Character.

Father, we belong to You. Lord, we surrender to You. Father, we submit every area of our house, family, and legacy over to You. Father, we belong to You.

In Jesus' Name. Amen.

## Day 17

## WAR TOGETHER

*For we wrestle not against flesh and blood, but against principalities, against powers, against the rulers of the darkness of this world, against spiritual wickedness in high places.*

EPHESIANS 6:12 KJV

Notice what Ephesians 6:12 KJV declares, "For we wrestle not against flesh and blood." Notice that the keyword here is "We." Warfare is a team sport. Don't war alone. The enemy wants to isolate you in an attempt to get you to fight alone.

When you are in Christ, you are never alone. Hebrews 13:5 KJV declares, "Let your conversation be without covetousness; and be content with such things as ye have: for he hath said, I will never leave thee, nor forsake thee." God will never leave you or forsake you. Christ is with you always—He is Emmanuel, "God with us."

Never fight your battle without engaging God first. Never fight alone. Never fight in your own strength and capacity. Zechariah 4:6 KJV declares, "Then he answered and spake unto me, saying, This is the word of the Lord unto Zerubbabel, saying, Not by might, nor by power, but by my spirit, saith the Lord of hosts." It's not by strength, nor by power, nor by human capability, or intellect, that you'll win spiritual wars. Spiritual wars are won through God.

God saw your battle before it began. He saw the situation before it formed. He saw the enemy's plan before it manifested. Remember that God is Omnipresent and Omniscient. He is everywhere at the same time. He occupies both space and time and He knows everything.

Revelation 1:8 KJV declares, "I am Alpha and Omega, the beginning and the ending, saith the Lord, which is, and which was, and which is to come, the Almighty." God exists outside of time. He existed before time began. In fact, eternity bows to Him. Time has no limits on God. Time obeys Him. Hebrews 11:3 KJV declares, "Through faith we understand that the worlds were framed by the word of God, so that things which are seen were not made of things which do appear." God's Word shaped and framed time itself.

According to Strong's Concordance, the Greek word for Worlds is *aiōn* (G165), which means "Period of time or age." God predates time itself. He shaped time and every dispensation. If God knows everything and He occupies time and space then why not engage Him in all things? Engage God in your daily affairs. Engage God in every battle. Engage God in every war. He knows the outcome before the battle begins. Go to the One who holds the answers in His Hands.

When you submit to God, He will lead and direct your footsteps. He will disarm the enemy's plot and ploy. When you engage God, He will direct and navigate your life's course. There is no battle that He cannot win. Fight the flesh with Christ.

John 1:14 KJV declares, "And the Word was made flesh, and dwelt among us, (and we beheld his glory, the glory as of the only begotten of the Father,) full of grace and truth." His Word became flesh and dwelt among us. Jesus Christ is God in the flesh. Jesus Christ led a perfect and sinless life in the flesh. The flesh is enmity against God. The flesh wars against God. Jesus Christ put on flesh in order to become our example. He dominated and ruled over sin and the flesh.

Romans 8:3 KJV declares, "For what the law could not do, in that it was weak through the flesh, God sending his own Son in the likeness of sinful flesh, and for sin, condemned sin in the flesh:" As the children of God, and joint-heirs with Jesus Christ, we have the power and authority to rule over sin—we have no excuse. Christ is with us. Christ lives in us. Christ wars for us and fights on our behalf. Christ leads us. Let Christ lead you. Let Christ lead your marriage.

This war is bigger than you. The battle is bigger than your purpose. The battle is bigger than your destiny. The battle is bigger than your marriage. This war is not of flesh and blood but against principalities, against powers, against the rulers of the darkness of this world, against spiritual wickedness in high places—the war is against the kingdom of darkness. Satan is after the institution of marriage.

Ever since the beginning, Satan was jealous of man. Notice in Genesis 1 what God had declared over man, "And God said, Let us make man in our image, after our likeness: and let them have dominion over the fish of the sea, and over the fowl of the air, and over the cattle, and over all the earth, and over every creeping thing that creepeth upon the earth. So God created man in his own image, in the image of God created he him; male and female created he them. And God blessed them, and God said unto them, Be fruitful, and multiply, and replenish the earth, and subdue it: and have dominion over the fish of the sea, and over the fowl of the air, and over every living thing that moveth upon the earth." Genesis 1:26–28 KJV. God gave man the authority to dominate over everything on the Earth — including Satan.

Interestingly enough, Satan was in the Garden of Eden and God gave man the authority to dominate over and subdue everything that creepeth on the Earth — including the snake that was in the Garden. God gave mankind the delegated spiritual and natural authority to rule over Satan and to lord over the Earth. However, when man disobeyed God, Adam gave up authority to lord over the Earth. Adam gave up lordship and Jesus Christ had to take it back for us. Matthew 28:18 KJV declares, "And Jesus came and spake unto them, saying, All power is given unto me in heaven and in earth."

Anyone who is in Christ has the authority to lead, rule, and dominate over anything that God has assigned to them. Psalms 24:1 KJV declares, "The earth is the Lord's, and the fulness thereof; the world, and they that dwell therein." The Earth belongs to God and He can delegate authority to whomever He pleases. Psalms 75:7 KJV declares, "But God is the judge: he putteth down one, and setteth up another." God raises up kings and sets down kingdoms. Through Christ you have the victory. Through Christ you have dominion.

Revelation 20:14 KJV declares, "And death and hell were cast into the lake of fire. This is the second death." The enemy knows his end. Satan knows that he will be defeated. Satan knew his demise even from the beginning. God spoke to Satan in the Garden, "And the Lord God said unto the serpent, Because thou hast done this, thou art cursed above all cattle, and above every beast of the field; upon thy belly shalt thou go, and dust shalt thou eat all the days of thy life: And I will put enmity between thee and the woman, and between thy seed and her seed; it shall bruise thy head, and thou shalt bruise his heel." Genesis 3:14–15 KJV.

In the Amplified Version, Genesis 3:14–15 AMPC declares, "And the Lord God said to the serpent, Because you have done this, you are cursed above all [domestic] animals and above every [wild] living thing of the field; upon your belly you shall go, and you shall eat dust [and what it contains] all the days of your life. And I will put enmity between you and the woman, and between your offspring and her Offspring; He will bruise and tread your head underfoot, and you will lie in wait and bruise His heel." Satan knew his demise from the beginning. Satan was dividing families and attacking marriages since the beginning of time.

God is a loving Father and will never lead you or your family astray. When you are in Christ, the entanglement of sin cannot keep you hostage. When you are in Christ, the power of sin has no authority over you or your marriage. Jesus Christ is our example and He dominated over sin and reconciled us back to God the Father. Jesus Christ reconciled our Covenant with God, through His shed Blood.

"Having abolished in his flesh the enmity, even the law of commandments contained in ordinances; for to make in himself of twain one new man, so making peace; And that he might reconcile both unto God in one body by the Cross, having slain the enmity thereby: And came and preached peace to you which were afar off, and to them that were nigh. For through him we both have access by one Spirit unto the Father." Ephesians 2:15–18 KJV.

God's Word is stronger than the battle that you face. Your spouse is not your enemy. Unity breaks generational cycles. Choose to fight the enemy in every area of your life together. "For we wrestle not against flesh and blood, but against principalities, against powers, against the rulers of the darkness of this world, against spiritual wickedness in high places." Ephesians 6:12 KJV. Choose to war together. Choose to build together.

## ACTION

- Today, choose not to argue. The war is not with your spouse.
- Be deliberate on keeping peace within the borders of your home. Let the Peace of God flourish within your communication, both verbal and nonverbal.
- Choose to disengage from foul and corrupt communication and choose to engage God.
- Pray and ask God to soften your heart and let God lead your language.
- Remember that your spouse is not the enemy. Choose to engage His Peace in times of chaos. Engage His Grace in times of turmoil.

## Day 18

# KILL THE SNAKE

> *Now the serpent was more subtil than any beast of the field which the Lord God had made. And he said unto the woman, Yea, hath God said, Ye shall not eat of every tree of the garden?*
>
> GENESIS 3:1 KJV

According to Strong's Concordance, the Hebrew word for Subtil is *aruwm* (H6175), which means "Shrewd, sly, sensible, or crafty." Satan is crafty. Satan likes to manipulate. The enemy likes to craft cunning circumstances within the walls of your life and marriage. Satan wants to contaminate your garden by getting you to disobey or doubt God's Word. Genesis 3:1 AMPC declares, "Now the serpent was more subtle and crafty than any living creature of the field which the Lord God had made. And he [Satan] said to the woman, Can it really be that God has said, You shall not eat from every tree of the garden?"

Notice in Genesis 3:1 AMPC, Satan stated, "Can it really be that God has said, You shall not eat from every tree of the garden?" Satan will try to lure you into his way of thinking. Satan wants you to question God's Command. What assignment has God given you? In Genesis 2:17 KJV, God specifically gave an order to not eat of a specific tree, "But of the tree of the knowledge of good and evil, thou shalt not eat of it: for in the day that thou eatest thereof thou shalt surely die."

Satan and his way of doing things is enmity against God and wars against what God has said. Satan wars against God's Word. Satan is cunning and he wedges himself in between what God has said and your human logic. Notice that Satan was on or near the one thing that God told them not to touch. Satan wants proximity.

Why was Eve near the tree that God told them not to eat from? Satan wants to lure you. Satan wants to entice you. Satan tricks. Satan manipulates. Satan will draw you into areas that God has commanded you not to touch. Do not give Satan access or proximity to your destiny. Do not give Satan proximity to your promise. Your home, marriage, and family is your God-given Garden. Do not give Satan access to any area of it. Cast him out of every area of your marriage. Guard your marriage with all diligence, tend to it, and keep it with the Word of God.

When Satan speaks, use the Word of God to defeat Him. Remember how Jesus defeated Satan in the wilderness?"And when the tempter came to him, he said, If thou be the Son of God, command that these stones be made bread. But he answered and said, It is written, Man shall not live by bread alone, but by every word that proceedeth out of the mouth of God." Matthew 4:3–4 KJV. Every time Satan tried to tempt Jesus, Christ used the Word to silence and to destroy the enemy's plan. Kill the snake's communication. Kill and disarm the enemy's plan by using the Word of God.

Genesis 2:15 KJV declares, "And the Lord God took the man, and put him into the garden of Eden to dress it and to keep it." Man's assignment was to steward the garden and to "keep it."

According to Strong's Concordance, the Hebrew word for Keep is *shamar* (H8104), which means "To guard, observe, give heed, to have charge of, keep watch and ward, protect, and watchman." God gave man the authority to serve as a watchman over the Garden. The snake was trespassing. It was man's responsibility to "guard the Garden" with the Word of God.

In Genesis 2, God's Word to Adam and Eve was, "Don't touch." Let the Word of God set the moral and spiritual parameters of your home. Don't let the enemy breach your covenant. Kill Satan's paralytic impact on your heart, marriage, and home. Satan wants to slow you down and stunt your destiny. When you are in Christ, you have the authority to crush every cunning snare, tactic, and trick of the enemy.

Luke 10:19 KJV declares, "Behold, I give unto you power to tread on serpents and scorpions, and over all the power of the enemy: and nothing shall by any means hurt you." When you are in Christ, Satan has no authority, or power over you, or your marriage. God has given you the authority and power to tread over all the power of the enemy.

According to Strong's Concordance, the Greek word for Tread is *pateō* (G3961), which means "To advance by setting foot upon." God has given you the authority to tread upon Satan and advance upon his kingdom. Let every aspect of your life tread upon the kingdom of darkness. Your marriage was designed to reflect the Love of Christ, and through it, you are to advance the Kingdom of God by setting your foot upon the enemy's head.

With every step that you take together, you're advancing on and conquering over Satan's kingdom — take new ground for the Kingdom of God. This is the reason why Satan wants to divide your marriage. Satan thrives in division, confusion, and chaos. If Satan can divide your home then he can slow you down from fulfilling your purpose and impact your family's legacy. Satan wants to derail you, your marriage, and every person attached to your purpose. Division and divorce have a ripple effect on everyone involved.

Divorce does not only impact you, the husband and wife, divorce has a devastating generational spiritual, emotional, physical, mental, and financial effect on everyone attached to you. Divorce separates. Divorce weakens the familial infrastructure. Divorce weakens the weapon of the family. Divorce has a devastating consequence on generational legacy.

Remember that Satan is cunning. Satan wants to infiltrate upon the ground of your home. He will try to gain access to any area that you give him permission to enter. Don't give the enemy access to your life or your marriage. Satan wants access. Choose to close every open door. Kill the enemy in every area of your life. When Satan speaks, deliberately shut him down with the Word of God.

Build your spiritual arsenal by studying and meditating on His Word day and night together. Joshua 1:8 KJV declares, "This book of the law shall not depart out of thy mouth; but thou shalt meditate therein day and night, that thou mayest observe to do according to all that is written therein: for then thou shalt make thy way prosperous, and then thou shalt have good success."

The Amplified Version expounds upon Joshua 1:8 AMPC in the following manner, "This Book of the Law shall not depart out of your mouth, but you shall meditate on it day and night, that you may observe and do according to all that is written in it. For then you shall make your way prosperous, and then you shall deal wisely and have good success." Follow the Word of God and you'll have good success. Submit to the Word of God within the walls of your marriage and you'll have good success.

Success is a choice. Choose to conquer the enemy together. Choose to fight the enemy together. Choose to keep your life and marriage clean. Choose to kill the snake in every area of your life. Choose to resist the enemy's temptations, lusts, traps, snares, and entanglements.

Remember snakes are only dangerous if you let them get close. Snakes want proximity. Snakes sneak their way into your life so that they can strike and poison you with their venom. After the snake's bite, the venom penetrates into your cardiovascular system and gets into your bloodstream, and ultimately paralyzes you. The snake can only bite you if you let it get close. Snakes want intimacy. They want to be unassuming. They are cunning and they are waiting and ready to strike in order to paralyze you, choke you, and swallow you whole. "So be subject to God. Resist the devil [stand firm against him], and he will flee from you." James 4:7 AMPC. Kill the snake and everything attached to it. Don't let the snake get close proximity to your life, heart, or family.

Lust is a snake. Lust lures you into its entanglement of deceit and lies. Lust will make you think that something or someone else is better than what you have today. Remember what Satan told Eve in Genesis 3:4–5 KJV, "And the serpent said unto the woman, Ye shall not surely die: For God doth know that in the day ye eat thereof, then your eyes shall be opened, and ye shall be as gods, knowing good and evil." Lust is tied to deceit, perversion, and manipulation. Deceit will look like the truth until it bites you. Lust wants to paralyze you and deceit is filled with empty promises.

Eve spoke back to Satan and said, "We may eat of the fruit of the trees of the garden: But of the fruit of the tree which is in the midst of the garden, God hath said, Ye shall not eat of it, neither shall ye touch it, lest ye die." Genesis 3:2–3 KJV.

Notice, in Genesis 3:1 KJV Satan perverts God's Word, "Now the serpent was more subtil than any beast of the field which the Lord God had made. And he said unto the woman, Yea, hath God said, Ye shall not eat of every tree of the garden?" Satan wants to pervert the Word that you have inside of you. Choose to study the Word of God. Get stronger in the Word so that you can fight the good fight of faith. Don't let the enemy contaminate the Word that's already in you. Choose to believe what God has declared.

Remember, snakes want proximity and they want access to your life. Satan got close enough to Eve in order to gain access to her thoughts and to her heart. Notice that Eve revealed to Satan what was in her heart. Genesis 3:2–3 declares, "And the woman said unto the serpent, We may eat of the fruit of the trees of the garden: But of the fruit of the tree which is in the midst of the garden, God hath said, Ye shall not eat of it, neither shall ye touch it, lest ye die." How you choose to use the Word of God reveals what's in your heart. How you choose to deploy the Word of God, as a weapon, reveals how deep the Word is rooted in your heart.

What's in your heart? Essentially what Satan asked Eve, in Genesis 3:1 KJV was, "Do you really believe what God said?" Lust lures and gets you to doubt the Word and the Promises of God. The enemy wants access so that he can pervert your thoughts and ultimately ruin your destiny.

Lust wants your destiny. Lust wants you to fall. Lust wants to ensnare you. Proverbs 2:16-20 KJV teaches us about lust in the form of the "Strange Woman". The Strange Woman is the personification of lust. In other words, replace the word "Strange Woman" with the word "Lust" and watch God unfold the assignment of lust to you.

Proverbs 2:16–20 KJV declares, "To deliver thee from the strange woman, even from the stranger which flattereth with her words; Which forsaketh the guide of her youth, and forgetteth the covenant of her God. For her house inclineth unto death, and her paths unto the dead. None that go unto her return again, neither take they hold of the paths of life. That thou mayest walk in the way of good men, and keep the paths of the righteous."

Lust lures. Lust has no limits. Lust has no boundaries. Lust tries to attach itself to both men and women. Lust is not just sexual sin, but it is also emotional, physical, mental, spiritual, and financial temptation and manipulation.

Who are you attached to? Why are you attached to them? Who is manipulating your heart? Who is leveraging your heart? Who or what is connected to your God-given resources? Who has your ear? Are your so-called friends' conversation emotionally luring you away? Emotional adultery is the same as committing the sexual act. Lust lures your heart away and the end result is death, destruction, and decay of destiny.

"For by means of a whorish woman a man is brought to a piece of bread: and the adulteress will hunt for the precious life." Proverbs 6:26 KJV. Kill the snake. Kill lust. Kill its assignment. Lust destroys. Lust lures. Lust wants your destiny. Lust wants your family. Lust wants your marriage. Lust wants what you're trying to build. Choose to divorce lust.

"For the lips of a strange woman drop as an honeycomb, and her mouth is smoother than oil: But her end is bitter as wormwood, sharp as a twoedged sword. Her feet go down to death; her steps take hold on hell. Lest thou shouldest ponder the path of life, her ways are moveable, that thou canst not know them. Hear me now therefore, O ye children, and depart not from the words of my mouth. Remove thy way far from her, and come not nigh the door of her house: Lest thou give thine honour unto others, and thy years unto the cruel: Lest strangers be filled with thy wealth; and thy labours be in the house of a stranger; And thou mourn at the last, when thy flesh and thy body are consumed, And say, How have I hated instruction, and my heart despised reproof; And have not obeyed the voice of my teachers, nor inclined mine ear to them that instructed me! I was almost in all evil in the midst of the congregation and assembly. Drink waters out of thine own cistern, and running waters out of thine own well. Let thy fountains be dispersed abroad, and rivers of waters in the streets. Let them be only thine own, and not strangers' with thee. Let thy fountain be blessed: and rejoice with the wife of thy youth. Let her be as the loving hind and pleasant roe; let her breasts satisfy thee at all times; and be thou ravished always with her love. And why wilt thou, my son, be ravished with a strange woman, and embrace the bosom of a stranger?" Proverbs 5:3–20 KJV.

Run from lust. Run far from its venomous sting. Snakes, whorish men, and strange women want proximity and access to your life. Lust is after your marriage. Lust is after your garden. Keep your garden clean, safe, and secure with the Word of God.

Choose to guard the garden of your heart, your marriage, and your family by submitting to the Word of God. Song of Solomon 2:15 KJV declares, "Take us the foxes, the little foxes, that spoil the vines: for our vines have tender grapes." It's the little foxes that spoil the vine. It's the little things that corrupt your marriage. Guard and keep your marriage. Protect your family. Honor God and preserve your legacy.

## ACTION

- Decide to keep your house clean and pure from outside contaminants. Keep the snakes out. Identify the snakes together. Don't let the enemy's poisonous words infiltrate your home.

- Emotional lust is the same as physical adultery. Who are you emotionally connected to outside of your marriage? Who has your ear? Who has your heart?

- Emotional entanglement is the same as physical entrapment. Divorce the soul tie. Who is your soul connected to? Repent, forgive, and keep your covenant pure and clean.

- Forgive yourself, forgive one another, and move forward together.

## Day 19

# BUILD TOGETHER

*And if a kingdom be divided against itself, that kingdom cannot stand. And if a house be divided against itself, that house cannot stand.*

MARK 3:24–25 KJV

A kingdom divided will not stand. The enemy wants you to argue and debate against each other. The enemy wants your house divided. Division is the environment for chaos and confusion. "For God is not the author of confusion, but of peace." 1 Corinthians 14:33 KJV.

God is the Author and Creator of Peace. Notice, in Genesis Chapter 2, before sin entered the Garden, peace, and prosperity reigned within its borders. Where there is peace, productivity is near. Where there is peace, safety, and freedom are nearby.

Notice Adam's response to God in the Garden of Eden, after he had sinned: "And he said, Who told thee that thou wast naked? Hast thou eaten of the tree, whereof I commanded thee that thou shouldest not eat? And the man said, The woman whom thou gavest to be with me, she gave me of the tree, and I did eat." Genesis 3:11–12 KJV. After sin entered the garden, the blame game begins.

Adam declares in Genesis 3:12 KJV, "The woman whom thou gavest to be with me caused me to sin." Division will cause you to blame others for your lack of leadership. Division will cause you to blame others for your lack of submission and obedience to God's Word. Obedience is a choice. Peace is a choice. Leadership is a choice. Submission is a choice.

Who are you submitted to? Are you submitted to God or Satan? Are you enslaved to the opinions of people? Adam had his marching orders from God. The Command from God was to dominate, keep, and protect everything under his stewardship — even his family.

Husbands, as the head of the home and your family's spiritual covering, you are responsible for submitting to God even when it's not popular. God has entrusted the weight of the family to you. God will not give you more than you can handle.

A submitted father and husband will righteously rule as God leads his heart. Righteous leadership creates an environment of peace, prosperity, and productivity. Proverbs 29:2 NLT declares, "When the godly are in authority, the people rejoice. But when the wicked are in power, they groan."

When peace flourishes in your home, productivity reigns. When peace reigns in your home — diligence, and execution can flourish. As the spiritual head of the family, God has given you the authority to block and break generational bondages and cycles that try to impede your family's success and growth. Satan wants to derail your family from moving forward in purpose. Satan wants you to move from the Garden, into the wilderness, and into the place of bondage.

As the head of the home, God has given you the spiritual, emotional, financial, mental, and physical authority to break generational bondages and cycles. Just like Adam, you have the opportunity to either obey or disobey God. Choose to obey God. Choose to dominate in the Garden by obeying God's Command. Choose to dominate with your family. Let forgiveness flourish from your lips. Let peace rule within your heart.

Choose to lead, not as a dictator or as an overbearing taskmaster, but choose to lead your family according to knowledge. Lead them according to your intimate knowledge about them. Lead them according to the wisdom, understanding, and discernment that God has given you. Lead your family as a submitted Disciple under God's Direction.

Let your words be filled with His Character. Let your private life reflect the Heart of God. Let your public life reflect His Fruit. A contaminated private life will soon collapse upon itself. You may desire the public manifestation of family success and prosperity, but your private life is full of dead men's bones. Private sanctification is required for public exaltation. Humble yourself. Let God lead and order your steps.

Don't raise a generation of hypocrites. "Woe to you, scribes and Pharisees, pretenders (hypocrites)! For you are like tombs that have been whitewashed, which look beautiful on the outside but inside are full of dead men's bones and everything impure. Just so, you also outwardly seem to people to be just and upright but inside you are full of pretense and lawlessness and iniquity." Matthew 23:27–28 AMPC.

Obey God and build your house how God commands you to build. Build according to His Word. Build with God. Build with your spouse. Build together as one unit. "And if one prevail against him, two shall withstand him; and a threefold cord is not quickly broken." Ecclesiastes 4:12 KJV. Choose to not be easily broken.

When chaos is present, division and deterioration are near. Proverbs 29:18 KJV declares, "Where there is no vision, the people perish: but he that keepeth the law, happy is he." When there is no unified, God-given vision, the people perish. When there is no Godly vision, the people wither. A divided house produces a withered and powerless family. Division brings about a withered generation. What type of generation are you leading? Who are you stewarding? Who are you leading? How are you leading them? How are you stewarding the gifts that God has given you?

Matthew 7:24–27 KJV declares, "Therefore whosoever heareth these sayings of mine, and doeth them, I will liken him unto a wise man, which built his house upon a rock: And the rain descended, and the floods came, and the winds blew, and beat upon that house; and it fell not: for it was founded upon a rock. And every one that heareth these sayings of mine, and doeth them not, shall be likened unto a foolish man, which built his house upon the sand: And the rain descended, and the floods came, and the winds blew, and beat upon that house; and it fell: and great was the fall of it." What type of foundation are you building on? Who are you building on? Who are you building with? A house built on the Word of God will stand for generations to come. A house that's built on God's Word will stand the test of time.

Psalms 112:1–3 KJV declares, "Blessed is the man that feareth the Lord, that delighteth greatly in his commandments. His seed shall be mighty upon earth: the generation of the upright shall be blessed. Wealth and riches shall be in his house: and his righteousness endureth for ever." It's your choice to fear and revere God's Word. As a family, it is your choice to either be a family that reflects the Heart of God and flourish or you can choose to wander in the wilderness and wither.

After Adam and Eve were sent to the wilderness by God, in the next Chapter, Genesis 4, we can see the manifestation of sin due to Adam and Eve's disobedience. Through the story of Cain and Abel, we can see the manifestation of a generational cycle of sin. Your disobedience does not just impact you, it impacts everyone and everything that's attached to you. Although Adam and Eve were still alive, they were stripped of their authority. Sin will have you toiling in the wilderness. Don't toil. Choose to flourish.

The next generation wasn't born under The Promise — Cain and Abel were born in the wilderness, underneath the weight of sin. Cain and Abel operated under a new framework — the law of sin:

"Now Adam had sexual relations with his wife, Eve, and she became pregnant. When she gave birth to Cain, she said, "With the Lord's help, I have produced a man!" Later she gave birth to his brother and named him Abel. When they grew up, Abel became a shepherd, while Cain cultivated the ground. When it was time for the harvest, Cain presented some of his crops as a gift to the Lord. Abel also brought a gift — the best portions of the firstborn lambs from his flock. The Lord accepted Abel and his gift, but he did not accept Cain and his gift. This made Cain very angry, and he looked dejected. "Why are you so angry?" the Lord asked Cain. "Why do you look so dejected? You will be accepted if you do what is right. But if you refuse to do what is right, then watch out! Sin is crouching at the door, eager to control you. But you must subdue it and be its master." One day Cain suggested to his brother, "Let's go out into the fields." And while they were in the field, Cain attacked his brother, Abel, and killed him." Genesis 4:1–8 NLT.

Even though the framework of sin reigned, Cain and Abel still had a choice. They had a choice to either serve God or to be controlled by sin. Choose to be led by God and not controlled by sin.

Look at the stages of sin. Sin started with a small open door, Adam and Eve's disobedience in the Garden. Sin caused mankind to be stripped of their power, influence, and authority. Instead of flourishing in their God-given Purpose, in the Garden, they were sent to wither in the wilderness.

It was in the wilderness where the next generation was born. Your obedience, or disobedience, today, will determine where the next generation will be born. The choice is yours — obey God and flourish or disobey His Commandments and toil in the wilderness. Sin caused their family to toil for generations in the wilderness.

The full maturation of sin is death. Yes, Cain was jealous of Abel. Yes, Cain was angry at God. Cain was manipulative. Cain was vindictive, but the ultimate assignment of sin is death. Cain killed Abel. Cain had a choice. You have a choice. "Then when lust hath conceived, it bringeth forth sin: and sin, when it is finished, bringeth forth death." James 1:15 KJV.

The sin of one impacts the spiritual lineage of many. Your sin has consequence. Choose to eliminate the cycle of sin within your family's bloodline by choosing to obey God. Surrender to Christ and submit to Him. When you surrender to Christ, you have the choice to begin again. You can start afresh in Christ. Those who are in Christ have the opportunity to build something new.

Your spiritual DNA instantly changes when you're in Christ. The old habits, hang-ups, pitfalls, and snares of the past are over. When you are in Christ, He gives you the power to conquer your family's old way of doing things and follow His Pattern. You have the choice to establish a new pattern or you can bow to the gods, entanglements, and strongholds of the world. Choose Christ. Choose His Way.

# MY DECLARATION OVER YOUR FAMILY AND MARRIAGE

In the Name of Jesus, be set free from every bondage and stronghold of the past. Let Christ break every generational yoke and bondage. Let Christ rule within the confines of your family and home. Let His Peace overtake you. Let His Peace cover your marriage. Let His Joy fill every area of your home. Let His Word flourish within the confines of your home. Let His Power, Wisdom, and Insight dwell richly in every area of your life and marriage.

Let His Grace shower your lips. Let His Love be reflected in your communication. Let everything that your hands touch be Blessed. Let Favor shower your home. Let the Love of God and His Peace comfort you. Let every trap and snare of the enemy be exposed and destroyed by the Word and Power of God. Let the plot of the enemy have no power over your life and marriage. Let the power of the enemy be dethroned from within the walls of your marriage. Let the Power of God be exalted in every area of your life.

Let every stronghold and struggle be cast down. Let every memory of the past sin be wiped away. Let forgiveness reign and flourish within the heart of your marriage. Let forgiveness flow freely from your lips. Let the Character of God shine within the borders of your home. Let your seed be Blessed. Let your children's children be Blessed. Let your marriage be Blessed. Let God's Light shine on you and your family for generations to come. Let your generational bloodline be changed and transformed forever.

In the Name of Jesus, let the stain of sin be broken from your family's bloodline. Let the past be buried and be remembered no more. Let your house flourish. Let your house flow with witty ideas and inventions. Let the Blessings of the Lord overtake you and your house.

Blessed are you in the city, and blessed are you in the field. Blessed shall be the fruit of your body, and the fruit of your ground. Let every idea that comes out of you be Blessed. Let everything that your hands touch be Blessed. Let everything under your family's stewardship expand, enlarge, and increase. Let God enlarge your borders continually. Let God increase your capacity to handle more. May God increase your capability to do more.

May you find favor as you come in and go out. May you find favor even with your enemies. May the Lord cause your enemies that rise up against you to be smitten and crushed before thy face. They shall come out against thee one way, and flee before thee seven ways. May He make your enemies your footstool. May He make your feet like hind's feet and cause you to walk in high places.

May He make your family a Holy people unto Himself. May He establish you. May He increase you. May all the people of the Earth see that thou art called by the Name of the Lord, and they shall be afraid of thee. May He make you plenteous in goods. May He Bless your thoughts. May He Bless your ideas. May He Bless the fruit of your womb. May He Bless your womb.

May the Lord open unto thee His good treasure and open the heaven to give rain unto thy land in His season. May His Blessings overtake you. May He promote you. May He put your name in the mouth of kings. May He Bless all the work of your hands and thou shalt lend unto many nations, and thou shalt not borrow. May the Lord make you the head and not the tail. May you be above only, and not beneath.

May He open your ears to understand His Word. May He soften your heart to follow His Word. May you hearken unto the Commandments of the Lord thy God, which I command thee this day, to observe and to faithfully do them. May you be a hearer and doer of His Word forever.

In Jesus' Name. Amen.

## Day 20

# SEND THE WORD

> *And when Jesus was entered into Capernaum, there came unto him a centurion, beseeching him, And saying, Lord, my servant lieth at home sick of the palsy, grievously tormented. And Jesus saith unto him, I will come and heal him. The centurion answered and said, Lord, I am not worthy that thou shouldest come under my roof: but speak the word only, and my servant shall be healed. For I am a man under authority, having soldiers under me: and I say to this man, Go, and he goeth; and to another, Come, and he cometh; and to my servant, Do this, and he doeth it. When Jesus heard it, he marvelled, and said to them that followed, Verily I say unto you, I have not found so great faith, no, not in Israel.*
>
> MATTHEW 8:5–10 KJV

According to Strong's Concordance, the Greek word for Capernaum is *Kapharnaoum* (G2584), which means a village of comfort. Your family is a village and a place of comfort. In Matthew 8:5 KJV, Jesus entered into Capernaum — the dwelling place of comfort. Let Christ dwell in your home. Let your home be established as the "place of comfort." Let your home be declared as the "place of peace," where Christ can dwell. Let Christ dwell in the borders of your home.

When Christ enters the situation, miracles, signs, and wonders take place. In Matthew 8:5 KJV, Jesus Christ, God in the Flesh, walks into Capernaum — the village or place of comfort, and there came unto him a centurion, searching for Him, and stated, "Lord, my servant lieth at home sick of the palsy, grievously tormented." Notice that the Centurion met Christ in Capernaum in the "place of comfort". The Centurion's circumstance was certainly not a place of comfort.

In fact, the Centurion stated, "Lord, my servant lieth at home sick of the palsy, grievously tormented." The Centurion was experiencing discomfort — his servant was grievously tormented. Look at the dichotomy outlined here in Matthew 8:5 KJV. You have the Living Word of God, Jesus Christ, who is in a place of comfort — Capernaum, while this Centurion was experiencing torment and discomfort.

Notice what type of man approached Jesus — a Centurion. In Roman times, a Centurion, was a man of position, authority, influence, and stature. Notice that the Centurion did not care about his position or stature when he needed help. When you need help, choose to surrender to God and He will satisfy you. The Centurion killed his pride and surrendered to Christ.

Notice how the Centurion approached Jesus in Matthew 8:5 KJV, the first word out of this influential man's mouth was, "Lord." The Centurion immediately called Jesus Christ "Lord." This man of authority positioned himself in a place of submission.

Remember, pride kills breakthrough. Pride kills marriages. When you need help, seek God and let Him lead you to Godly Counsel. Choose to kill pride. When you crush pride and surrender to God, here is God's response to the humble — Matthew 8:7 KJV declares, "And Jesus saith unto him, I will come and heal him." When you kill pride — healing comes.

If you want to heal your marriage, kill pride. If you want to heal your relationship, forgive and kill pride. If you want reconciliation, kill pride. If you want to heal your family, kill pride. If you want restoration, kill pride. The Centurion did not only kill pride, but he also sought God.

Matthew 7:7 KJV declares, "Ask, and it shall be given you; seek, and ye shall find; knock, and it shall be opened unto you:" Ask, seek, and knock. Ask God for the breakthrough. Ask God for the healing. Ask and surrender to God. Seek Him. Seek His face. Seek and search His Word for His answer.

Matthew 5:6 declares, "Blessed are they which do hunger and thirst after righteousness: for they shall be filled." Matthew 5:6 AMPC puts it this way, "Blessed and fortunate and happy and spiritually prosperous (in that state in which the born-again child of God enjoys His favor and salvation) are those who hunger and thirst for righteousness (uprightness and right standing with God), for they shall be completely satisfied!"

The Centurion searched for the answer and asked God for the solution. When the Centurion found Christ, the Solution, he honored Him and called Him "Lord." The Centurion did not treat Christ as common. The Centurion understood the spiritual authority that Jesus Christ held.

The Centurion declared in Matthew 8:9 KJV, "Lord, I am not worthy that thou shouldest come under my roof: but speak the word only, and my servant shall be healed. For I am a man under authority, having soldiers under me: and I say to this man, Go, and he goeth; and to another, Come, and he cometh; and to my servant, Do this, and he doeth it." The Centurion understood natural authority and knew that the spiritual Authority of Jesus Christ far exceeded and outranked the Centurion's natural influence, authority, and spiritual rank.

The Centurion knew that his problem needed a supernatural solution. The Centurion recognized the Authority of Jesus Christ and submitted to Him. Decide to recognize the Power of God and let Christ flow freely in your life. Let His Word flow freely in your home. Let His Word flow freely in your marriage. Let His Word build your family's life and destroy everything that's not like Him. Let God send the Word to your home.

If God's Will is already accomplished in Heaven, and it is, choose to be the family on Earth where His Will can flow to and through. Let His Will be accomplished in your marriage, family, and home. Let His Will be done in your home — your place of comfort. Choose to be "Capernaum". Let your house freely receive His Word like the Centurion.

Ask God to send the Word to your home. Let His Word flow freely within your situation. Let His Word flow freely within your marriage. Send His Word to your finances. Declare His Word over every area of your life. Let His Word resurrect every dead thing. Let His Word reconstruct anything that's been dismantled by the enemy. Let His Word flow freely and strengthen your faith. Choose to trust Christ. Choose to send the Word.

## Day 21

# AS FOR ME AND MY HOUSE... WE WILL SERVE THE LORD

*And if it seems evil to you to serve the Lord, choose for yourselves this day whom you will serve, whether the gods which your fathers served on the other side of the River, or the gods of the Amorites, in whose land you dwell; but as for me and my house, we will serve the Lord.*

JOSHUA 24:15 AMPC

Make the decision to serve God. Choose to let Christ rule within the borders of your heart. Let His Word flourish within your family's spiritual DNA. Let His Word transform the ground of your home. Let His Word become your family's foundation and framework. Choose to let the idols and entanglements of the past go. Decide to move forward in God. Don't put your trust in things — put your trust in Christ.

"Some trust in chariots, and some in horses: but we will remember the name of the Lord our God." Psalms 20:7 KJV. Some families may trust in material things, but as for you and your house, choose to trust in the Lord. "Trust in the Lord with all thine heart; and lean not unto thine own understanding. In all thy ways acknowledge him, and he shall direct thy paths. Be not wise in thine own eyes: fear the Lord, and depart from evil. It shall be health to thy navel, and marrow to thy bones." Proverbs 3:5–8 KJV. Let God lead your heart and marriage.

Whenever fear or doubt tries to raise its head in your life, choose to speak to it and cast it into the sea. Mark 11:23 KJV declares, "For verily I say unto you, That whosoever shall say unto this mountain, Be thou removed, and be thou cast into the sea; and shall not doubt in his heart, but shall believe that those things which he saith shall come to pass; he shall have whatsoever he saith."

Whenever you're feeling overwhelmed, and you feel as if the enemy is trying to surround you and swallow you whole, choose to declare the Word of God. "And when the servant of the man of God was risen early, and gone forth, behold, an host compassed the city both with horses and chariots. And his servant said unto him, Alas, my master! how shall we do? And he answered, Fear not: for they that be with us are more than they that be with them. And Elisha prayed, and said, Lord, I pray thee, open his eyes, that he may see. And the Lord opened the eyes of the young man; and he saw: and, behold, the mountain was full of horses and chariots of fire round about Elisha." 2 Kings 6:15–17 KJV. I pray that God opens your eyes. Understand and know that God is fighting for you.

"And Moses said unto the people, Fear ye not, stand still, and see the salvation of the Lord, which he will shew to you to day: for the Egyptians whom ye have seen to day, ye shall see them again no more for ever." Exodus 14:13 KJV. Fear not, stand still, and see the Salvation of the Lord.

I pray, that your heart is softened and that the hardened heart of the past is erased. I pray, that God gives you a new heart, for you, for your family, for your marriage, and for your legacy. "A new heart also will I give you, and a new spirit will I put within you: and I will take away the stony heart out of your flesh, and I will give you an heart of flesh." Ezekiel 36:26 KJV.

Mark 2:22 KJV puts it this way, "And no man putteth new wine into old bottles: else the new wine doth burst the bottles, and the wine is spilled, and the bottles will be marred: but new wine must be put into new bottles." It is my earnest desire that God gives your family and marriage a new wineskin. You cannot put new wine, new information, new revelation, new insight, and new ways of doing things into an old framework and mindset. "Therefore if any man be in Christ, he is a new creature: old things are passed away; behold, all things are become new." 2 Corinthians 5:17 KJV.

I pray that you embrace the new. From this day forward, choose to fight together. Choose to build together. Choose to love together. Choose to serve together. Choose to transform generations together.

"And if it seems evil to you to serve the Lord, choose for yourselves this day whom you will serve, whether the gods which your fathers served on the other side of the River, or the gods of the Amorites, in whose land you dwell; but as for me and my house, we will serve the Lord." Joshua 24:15 AMPC.

## ACTION

- Create a "Family Covenant" together. "And the Lord answered me, and said, Write the vision, and make it plain upon tables, that he may run that readeth it." Habakkuk 2:2 KJV.

- Separately, take some time to write down what you're believing God for. As you're writing, pray and ask God to lead your heart as you're making your list.
- When you're finished, come together as a family and share what you've written down.
- Write out a comprehensive list outlining all of your family's responses.
- Prayerfully combine the lists together and write down what you are believing in God for, together as a family unit.
- Ask God to give you wisdom on how to execute each item on the list together as a family unit.
- Write down Scriptures associated with each item on the list and confess these Scriptures regularly. Declare them throughout the day.
- Create a Family Mission Statement based on the Word of God. For starters, pick a Scripture in the Bible that you believe is relevant to your family. And then, focus your family on that verse throughout the day.
- As time passes, build upon this verse as times and seasons change. Use other Scriptures to build and strengthen your family, life, and marriage.
- Pray regularly, early, and often. Pray for each other and with each other frequently.
- Choose to engage God in every aspect of your life, family, and marriage.

# MY PRAYER FOR YOUR FAMILY AND MARRIAGE

Father God, in the Name of Jesus, I pray that the ground of your marriage is blessed. I pray that God transforms generations through you. I pray that God breaks every generational yoke, cycle, and curse within the walls of your family. I pray that God tears down every generational stronghold, struggle, and hidden trap of the enemy. I pray, that every hidden thing is consumed by the Fire of God. For our God is a consuming fire.

I pray that God burns up every secret thought and desire. I pray that God burns up hidden sin. I pray that depression flees from your borders and every mental disease is cast down. In the Name of Jesus, I pray that the spirit of infirmity is destroyed and it takes its grip from off of your family's bloodline. In the Name of Jesus, I speak life into the heart of your marriage. I pray that you have life more abundantly. With long life shall He satisfy you.

I pray that God heals you and sets you free. I pray that God strengthens you and prepares you to be His Light in the Earth. I pray that the Blood of Jesus Christ covers you and saturates your family. In the Name of Jesus, I declare that the spirit of perversion, every unclean spirit, and every weapon of the enemy is destroyed and dismantled from the boundaries and borders of your home. I pray that wealth and riches are in your house. Lord, send now prosperity.

I pray that God bless the fruitful work of your hands. I pray that God's Peace fills your borders. I pray that God fills your house with the finest of wheat. I pray that your family is clothed in Righteousness. I pray that your family is clothed in Wisdom. I pray that your family and every part of your Covenant is blessed beyond what you can think or imagine. May God forever bless the Covenant of your marriage.

"Now to Him Who, by (in consequence of) the [action of His] power that is at work within us, is able to [carry out His purpose and] do superabundantly, far over and above all that we [dare] ask or think [infinitely beyond our highest prayers, desires, thoughts, hopes, or dreams]" Ephesians 3:20 AMPC.

In Jesus' Name. Amen.

FOR MORE BOOKS VISIT
www.VanceKJackson.com

www.ingramcontent.com/pod-product-compliance
Lightning Source LLC
Chambersburg PA
CBHW030911080526
44589CB00010B/244